1

Living Waters

Signs of the Times

Anne Marie Mongoven, O.P., Ph.D.
Santa Clara University

Maureen Gallagher, Ph.D.

Liturgical Contributor
Rita Claire Dorner, O.P., Ph.D.
Santa Clara University

Consultants
The Reverend Gerard Sloyan
Jean Marie Hiesberger

General Editor
Eileen Anderson

TABOR®
PUBLISHING
Allen, Texas

D1451133

SPECIAL THANKS

The authors wish to gratefully acknowledge the contributions of Margaret LeClaire, SSF, Susan Weinheimer, SSF, Donna Brock, Sandy Mory, and Carol Brennan in the development of this guide.

NIHIL OBSTAT
Rev. Glenn D. Gardner, J.C.D.
Censor Liborum

IMPRIMATUR
† Most Rev. Charles V. Grahmann
Bishop of Dallas

February 20, 1992

The *Nihil Obstat* and *Imprimatur* are official declarations that the work contains nothing contrary to Faith and Morals. It is not implied thereby that those granting the *Nihil Obstat* and *Imprimatur* agree with the contents, statements, or opinions expressed.

Send all inquiries to:
Tabor Publishing
One DLM Park
Allen, Texas 75002

Printed in the United States of America

ISBN 0-7829-0013-5

1 2 3 4 5   96 95 94 93 92

Contents

Our Lives

God's Word

The Church

We Pray

These symbols represent the four signs of catechesis
as found in *The General Catechetical Directory*
and *The National Catechetical Directory*.

BACKGROUND FOR THE CATECHIST

An evening dinner was the occasion for formulating the concept of *Living Waters*. As often happens, good conversation with friends at a meal leads to enthusiasm. Our enthusiasm about catechetics and catechesis eventually led to pencil and paper and a real *turn* on the catechetical path. The turn was not sharp. It was a long curve, with lots of road signs along the way to guide us. But it was a turn in the road.

For the past few centuries catechists have all traveled on the same road. Or to use another analogy, they all worked out of the same architectural plan. The foundation of their building was theology. The walls were creed, sacraments, commandments, and prayer. Theology was the starting point of the catechesis.

By contrast, *Living Waters* begins with human experience, not theology. The foundation of the program is the conviction that God, the Holy Mystery, is always present in our daily lives. Every human experience is a possible experience of God. God cannot be known outside of or apart from human experience.

The foundation of the program is the conviction that God, the Holy Mystery, is always present in our daily lives.

The *Living Waters* program offers a catechetical process that summons the catechized to recognize according to their ability the depth-dimension of ordinary human experiences. It takes the human experiences of children seriously. It addresses youngsters from within their cultural framework, recognizing that God is present in all of creation and in all of the signs of the times. *Living Waters* develops a process of examining human experiences that the children can continue to use as they grow older.

God is present in all of creation and in all of the signs of the times.

Human experience, however, does not stand alone. *Living Waters* looks at human experience through the eyes and ears, touch and words of the church. What do the Scriptures tell us about a particular kind of human experience? How does the life, the teaching, and the social justice of the church relate to this experience? In what way are our liturgies celebrations of this experience? We look at our ordinary human experiences and consider how God's self-communication through the church and the world enlightens us as to the religious dimension of our experiences.

Sharing the Light of Faith points out the importance of experience in catechesis. It states: "Experience is of great importance in catechesis. Experiential learning, which can be considered a form of inductive

The goal of catechesis is to nurture and strengthen the faith of the catechetical community and each individual within it.

methodology, gives rise to concerns and questions, hopes and anxieties, reflections and judgments, which increase one's desire to penetrate more deeply into life's meaning." (176d) We believe that the church has both wisdom and grace to share with us as we interpret these daily events.

The *Living Waters* program takes its inspiration and scope from *Sharing the Light of Faith: National Catechetical Directory for Catholics of the United States* and *The General Catechetical Directory. Living Waters* embraces as its own the goal of catechesis set forth in those documents, namely, to help people's faith "become living, conscious, and active through the light of instruction." (GCD, art. 17) Faith is seen as a living reality, a vital compelling force in today's world just as it was two thousand years ago.

For Christians, faith is a human commitment to God through Jesus Christ and the power of the Spirit living with us. It is God's gift to us. Faith grows when nourished and weakens when neglected. The goal of catechesis is to nurture and strengthen the faith of the catechetical community and each individual within it. When teaching children, the goal is to initiate them fully and freely into the life of the church.

Living Waters aims to foster a personal and communal understanding of the faith necessary for a free and informed acceptance of what God calls us to be. It aims to lead the People of God, children and adults, individually and communally, to an expression of their faith commitment through prayer and service to the church and the world. It strives to give the catechetical community an intelligent understanding of the church's stories, beliefs, and values. Ultimately, the goal of the *Living Waters* catechetical program is to contribute to the maturity of faith in the Christian community.

The structure of the process used in *Living Waters* is new. It is true that most other catechetical series do begin lessons with the experience of the child and then reflect on that experience in the light of church tradition. But their structural organization begins with theology. The authors say, "What human experience can we go back to in order to present a particular theological point?" *Living Waters* asks, "What human experience of children of this age do we wish to examine, and what does our faith tell us about this experience?"

Catechesis with Living Waters *encourages and promotes critical reflection on human experiences.*

Living Waters examines and interprets life experiences in the light of faith. It leads the children to search for meaning, and it shares with them the church's understanding of reality through catechesis of the church's primary symbols. Catechesis with *Living Waters* encourages and promotes critical reflection on human experiences. It is convinced that only through critical reflection on the church's tradition will the catechetical community freely choose a life of faith.

In pain and in joy, in all our human experiences, God is with us.

Selected Principles of Curriculum Development

The authors of *Living Waters* believe that the loving and compassionate God whom Jesus preached is with us always. The human community is never without this Spirit-Presence that gives us hope. In our daily lives the Divine Mystery supports and encourages us as we work and play, as we grieve and love, as we give birth, and as we die. In pain and in joy, in all our human experiences, God is with us.

The curriculum of *Living Waters* developed from an understanding of human growth and development and from theological premises. The authors chose to develop a curriculum with freedom and flexibility, as well as one whose theological context is that of Roman Catholicism. In electing this framework the authors consciously determined to steer a middle course between a curriculum that attempts to socialize children into the Roman Catholic Church by indoctrination without regard for human freedom, and one that emphasizes moral growth and faith development independently of the traditions of the Roman Catholic community.

Thus the *Living Waters* program aims to guide children enrolled in catechetical programs on a way that leads to (1) critical thinking about the meaning of life, (2) communal and individual response to God, especially as revealed in the redeeming words and works of Jesus Christ, and (3) communal and individual awareness of the nature of the church and a desire for full membership within it. The program seeks to achieve these aims by introducing the youngsters to those signs and symbols that Roman Catholicism has traditionally regarded as revelatory of God's abiding presence in the world.

Children become aware of their responsibility for themselves, for others, and for the world in which they live.

In developing the curriculum certain principles were chosen to be incorporated within it. Some of the principles are:

- Catechesis begins with human experience and critically reflects on the meaning and value of that experience.

- Through examination of their experiences children become aware of their responsibility for themselves, for others, and for the world in which they live. They recognize that they are accountable to God for the way they relate to all of creation.

- The Catholic heritage is so rich and varied that a child can find it attractive and appealing and ultimately love the church as a force for justice, love, and freedom in the world.

Every catechetical endeavor must be mindful of the larger pursuit of ultimate meaning and purpose in human existence.

- One becomes Christian only in community. In catechesis the social dimensions of human experience and church life and teaching merit constant emphasis.

- The Christian mystery is an organic whole. While it is necessary for catechesis to focus on particulars and specific themes, these themes are not seen in isolation from one another. The hierarchy of truths as presented in *The General Catechetical Directory* and *Sharing the Light of Faith* are all part of the catechesis in this program.

- From the beginning, membership, beliefs, and practices are presented in such a way that it should never be necessary to "unteach," that is, correct false notions and compensate for erroneous concepts taught at an earlier age.

- Every catechetical endeavor must be mindful of the larger pursuit of ultimate meaning and purpose in human existence. One session or one chapter or one grade is only a part of the whole catechesis.

- Truth is served best by being sensitive to appropriate language. Inclusive language is used throughout the program. Traditional images such as God as "Father" and "the Kingdom of God" are used, though not exclusively, because of their prominence in the tradition.

- Multicultural inclusion and ecumenical sensitivity permeate the text.

- The realization that action for justice appears as a constitutive dimension of the Gospel is integral to the catechetical process. The catechesis urges not only the individual but the entire catechetical community to work for justice.

- Critical reflection on life experiences, the Scriptures, the church, and liturgical experiences is encouraged. Unless children become critical thinkers they cannot know the truth.

One fundamental principle, more important than all others, is the conviction that the catechist is more important than all other catechetical principles. The catechist is the minister of the church, the one who witnesses to faith, the one who expresses the church's care and the church's wisdom. The catechist is the one who invites faith from the children. Successful catechesis does not rest solely on books or audiovisual aids. The ultimate effect of catechesis depends on the catechist and on the grace of God.

The ultimate effect of catechesis depends on the catechist and on the grace of God.

Living Waters exists to support and nourish and strengthen the catechist. It exists to give the busy catechist ideas and organization and resources. The real Living Water for the children is the catechist as a visible witness of the faith of the church.

Catechesis for the Six-Year-Old Child

The central theme of the catechesis for first grade children is "Identity." Six-year-old children are seeking to identify themselves as individuals. They are moving from the world of family, child care, and kindergarten to the wider world of education. Who am I? How do I fit with this larger community? On whom can I count for love and support? These are some of the unarticulated questions of the children whom you serve as catechist.

Living Waters will help you, as a catechist in the Parish Religious Education program or in the Catholic School, to lead the children to examine their experiences of (1) naming, (2) being special, (3) hands, (4) ears, (5) eyes, and (6) life itself. These experiences are organized into six chapters:

1. Naming
2. Being Special
3. Hands Are for Helping
4. Ears Are for Hearing
5. Eyes Are for Seeing
6. Life Is Good

Each chapter is divided into four parts. First there is a reflection on the experience (life sign) of the child. In the second part (the biblical sign) the children look at biblical stories that help them understand something about themselves and their relation to God. The third part (the ecclesial sign) looks at the same experience from the point of view of the church's life, teaching, and acts of justice. And in the fourth part (the liturgical sign) the children discover how the church celebrates their experiences in liturgy.

Each chapter begins with a reflection on the life sign of the child. For one session or one week you will lead the children through stories, questions, and other activities that help them discover something about their identity. During the life-sign sessions there is no discussion of religious stories or truths. These sessions provide an opportunity for the children to consider themselves and how they live in the world. A full consideration of the life sign will give greater meaning to the other signs in the following session or weeks. This *Catechist Preparation Guide* will assist you in developing the life sign.

The second part, or biblical sign, invites the children to discover how their experiences are related to the experiences of biblical people, stories, or teaching. The question for you to keep in mind is, What do these biblical stories tell us about the life sign we are considering? Again, the guide will assist you in developing the biblical sign. It is in the biblical sign that the children meet Jesus. Here they will hear his words and learn his story. They will see that Jesus cared for children and that he experienced childhood just as they experience it.

The central theme of the catechesis for first grade children is "Identity."

A full consideration of the life sign will give greater meaning to the other signs in the following session or weeks.

The liturgical sign is a culmination of the previous three sessions.

You, as catechist, are asked to invite the children to prayer and to bless them.

The third part of each chapter, the ecclesial sign, invites the children to relate their experience to the life, the teaching, the witness of the church. The word *church* refers to the whole People of God, past and present. The question for you to keep in mind is, What does the church tell us about the life sign we are considering? Again, the guide will assist you in leading the children through this session.

The fourth part of each chapter, the liturgical sign, asks, How does the church celebrate this experience? The church celebrates visibly, tangibly, audibly, appealing to all the senses. It makes visible the love of God for us and gives us an opportunity to express our faith in the God we come together to worship. The liturgical sign is a culmination of the previous three sessions. The guide will help you lead this part.

Catechesis on each of the four signs closes with a prayer. The prayers are designed to involve the children as much as possible. You, as catechist, are asked to invite the children to prayer and to bless them. Christmas and Easter catechesis and celebrations are provided in the liturgy pages at the end of the book.

Besides the *Catechist Preparation Guide,* which is for study *before* the catechesis, an *Annotated Edition* of the child's book is available for use *during* the catechetical sessions. The *Annotated Edition* incorporates annotations on the pages of the child's book, offering suggestions for the catechist to use during the sessions. The aims for each session and the key points to remember are boxed on the appropriate pages of the *Annotated Edition.*

Living Waters also offers an opportunity for the children to review each chapter with "Remembering" pages at the end of each chapter. It may be a good idea to have the children complete these pages at home and bring them back to you at the beginning of the next chapter. Be sure to correct them and acknowledge each child's growth.

The "Family Matters" page at the beginning of each chapter offers an opportunity for the children and their families to consider what the child is doing and learning in catechesis. Encourage the families to use these pages.

Being an Effective Catechist

This *Catechist Preparation Guide* parallels the organization of the child's book. It presents six chapters, each of which is divided into four parts. The preparation for each part begins with a "Journeying in Faith" essay that gives you, as a catechist, experiential, theological, scriptural, or liturgical background. The essay takes your experiences seriously and asks you about their meaning in the light of your faith.

Each session with the children follows a plan, or a pattern of development. This plan is called "Journeying in Faith with Children." The plan begins with a "Gathering Together." This gathering time provides an opportunity for you to welcome the children and to establish relationships with them. It also provides time for the children to relate to one another. "Gathering Together" is a community-building time.

The second part of each session, "Sharing Together," is a time for sharing stories—the stories of God and God's people, or the stories, beliefs, values, and liturgies of the church. It is a time for learning and loving.

"Acting Justly," the third part of each session, motivates the children both as individuals and as a community to live Christian lives of justice. It teaches them that for Christians, justice is not an option but an obligation.

"Praying Together" is the culminating activity of each session. Here you and the children gather together in the prayer center and as an assembly praise, thank, and ask for God's help. In "Praying Together" you express your sorrow and your unity. You pray for all the people you have talked about earlier in the session, and for all who are in need.

As the leader or the presider of the "Praying Together" activity, your movements, your attitudes, your spirit of praise or thanksgiving will carry over to the children. When you proclaim the Gospel, even just one verse, speak clearly and slowly so the children can hear and reflect on it. When you bless the children, let your motions be large enough for them to see and your words clear enough for them to hear.

One final point. More than we realize, children are conditioned by the spaces and places they enter. Excitement and creativity flourish when spaces and places invite them to talk with one another comfortably and receptively. Your planning should include not only familiarity with the session plan but also ideas of how the spaces will encourage and emphasize communication. A spirit of flexibility and creativity regarding environment will greatly enhance your planning.

The essay takes your experiences seriously and asks you about their meaning in the light of your faith.

A spirit of flexibility and creativity regarding environment will greatly enhance your planning.

1. Naming

Joshua Shawna Cathy Darren Miles Charles Yolanda Joseph Roberto Tommy Sheila John Doug Tiffany Billy Steven Debbie Shelby Alberto Lian Maria Casandra Alice Phillip Ingrid Ronald Tyler Chian Rachel Pat Leon Glenn Aretha Leroy Angelo Tracy Erlo Scott Dollie Kimberly Christy Trini Lor Karen Jennifer

Looking Ahead

Do you know the story of your name? In this chapter we will find out how names tell who we are and what family we belong to. We will learn who named Jesus and what His name means.

Chapter Aims

OUR LIVES

To learn the meanings of the names that we are called: personal name, family name, nickname

GOD'S WORD

To learn from the Bible about the naming of John the Baptist and Jesus

THE CHURCH

To learn that we are called "children of God," "Christian," "Catholic"

WE PRAY

To appreciate the process of giving and receiving a name, especially in Baptism; to learn the Sign of the Cross as a naming prayer

---

Chapter One Theme Song

"My Name" from the cassette *Songs for Living Waters 1* by Stephen Chapin

---

Using the Chapter Title Page

Before you begin Part One, invite the children to look with you at page 5, the Title Page of Chapter One. Read together the chapter title and the names that appear there. Invite each child to see if his or her own name appears on the page.

Help the children to look ahead to the content of the chapter by asking the question that appears in the "Looking Ahead" box. Then preview the chapter by reading the rest of that paragraph to them. Introduce yourself by printing your name on the chalkboard or on a piece of posterboard.

Chapter Plan Ahead

Make arrangements for the following items well in advance of the part of the chapter in which they are used:

- Obtain a bare tree limb to place in a container of sand or dirt. This will be called the "Naming Tree." (Part 1)

- Check the meanings of the names of the children from an authoritative book on names. (Part 2)

- Arrange for the visit to the baptistry in the church and check on the availability of a priest or deacon to talk with the children about baptism. (Part 4)

- Order and preview the suggested audiovisual material. (Parts 2 and 4)

Audiovisual References

The First Christmas, VHS, from The Children's Video Bible series, Credence Cassettes, 115 E. Armour Blvd., Kansas City, MO 64141 (Part 2)

Baptism—We Belong to God's Family, VHS, from Sacred Heart Kid's Club series, Don Bosco Multimedia, 475 North Ave., Box T, New Rochelle, NY 10802–0845 (Part 4)

Music for the Prayer Services

"We Are Walking in the Light" from the *Hymnal for Catholic Students,* #199.

PART ONE
WHAT IS YOUR NAME?

Our Lives

We want our name to be respected because our name stands for us. How do you feel when someone you love calls you by name?

What a wonderful treasure it is to know the story of your naming. Do you know why your parents named you as they did?

Journeying in Faith

Have you ever really thought about your name?

Our names are precious to us. We identify ourselves with them. We like to hear them said in a loving way. We want our name to be respected because our name stands for us.

Not everyone calls us by name. Only those who know us and with whom we are on a friendly basis call us by our name. Until a name is known, a person remains a stranger. Even when we do not personally know someone, if we know his or her name, we have some knowledge of the person. Naming is the first step in knowing.

Your first name gives you a sense of personal identity. It sets you apart from the other members of your family. It signifies your individuality.

Your full name stands for you. It identifies you to others. When you sign your name, you are responsible for what you sign. Your signature on a bank loan commits you to the terms of the contract. When you accomplish something, your name is given honor. It is written on diplomas and certificates. Your name stands for you.

We do not choose our own names. Others name us. Parents name their children. They choose names for different reasons. Sometimes, children are named after relatives, persons their parents admire, or popular figures in society.

Do you know the story of your naming? Why did your parents name you as they did? What a wonderful treasure it is to know the story of your naming. Be sure to tell children in your family the reasons for their names.

We share our family name with those we love. The family name shared with children notifies both the children and society that these children are members of this family. Family names give a sense of belonging. They relate us to others. They indicate that we are not alone in society. Others share our name and our lives.

Family names give us a past. In ancient times, people identified themselves as belonging to a tribe or nation. Surnames emerged in the Middle Ages. They were given to distinguish one family from another. The family name might derive from the trade of the father: Smith, Baker, Taylor. It might describe the place where the family lived: Dale, Hill, Lee, Lake. Sometimes the family name simply identified the father: Johnson, Williamson, Erickson. Girls were also named after their father. Kristin Lavransdatter was the daughter of Lavrans. Surnames always indicated relationship.

Do you have a nickname? How do you feel about it?

Have you ever been called by a nickname? Some people have nicknames. A nickname is a name added to or substituted for the proper name. To nickname someone is to describe a basic feature or characteristic of the person. Nicknames may describe a part of the body, such as Curly, Slim, Blondie, or Shorty. At other times, a nickname may describe an accomplishment of the person, such as Buffalo Bill.

Occasionally, nicknames became surnames: Armstrong, Ironside, Whitehead, Lightfoot. Nicknames may simply be a shortened form of the Christian name, such as Tom, Beth, Will, or Meg. Sometimes, nicknames are signs of endearment, such as Princess, Sonny, Honey, or Dolly.

When we call persons by a number or substitute a number for their name, we dehumanize them. In our computerized society, people often reject being identified by number. We need to be called by our name.

Family names give a sense of belonging. They relate us to others.

We do not like to think of ourselves as mastering or controlling other people. Yet by naming them, we do so. Children identify with the name we give them. As part of the family, they absorb the values, attitudes, and world view of those who name them. By naming others, we become in some sense responsible for them.

Today surnames often indicate ancestry. Italian, Hispanic, Irish, and German names identify a person with a society. Many black citizens in the United States are choosing African names as a sign of their pride in their ancestry.

Write down in a column all the names that you are called. For example, Mrs. Smith may also be called Officer Smith, Margaret, Maggie, Mummy, Maggie Winslow, Jimmy's mother, Margaret Winslow-Smith, and so on.

Write here some of the names you are called.

Next to each name, write down one word that shows how you feel or what you think of when you are called by each name of yours. For example, Officer Smith may elicit "respect" and Mummy may bring to mind "love."

Look at your names and your responses. How does this "naming" picture of you make you feel?

Journeying in Faith with Children

OUR LIVES

Aims

- To recognize how unique each name is
- To recognize that family names show relationship
- To learn about nicknames
- To find out who can give a name

New Words

name
nickname

Materials

Day 1: • crayons or markers
   • name cards
   • yarn or string
   • Naming Tree
Day 2: • crayons or markers
   • paper rectangles
Day 3: • drawing paper
   • crayons
Day 4: • stuffed animal
   • large sheets of butcher paper (optional)

Theme Song

"My Name" from the cassette *Songs for Living Waters 1* by Stephen Chapin

Day 1

◆ **Gathering Together.**   Have the children form a circle. Call each child by name and present him or her with a book. When all have their books, have them hold their books up and then bless them, saying: "God, bless these books and bless these special children whom you have called by name." Have the children respond with "Amen."

◆ **Sharing Together.**   Encourage everyone to look through the books and to comment on the cover and illustrations. Have the children turn to pages 6 and 7 and look at all the happy children smiling at them. Mention that these are our new friends. We will get to know their names. We will get to know so many stories about them!

• As everyone looks at page 7, pass out crayons or markers and have the children print their first names and draw in the space provided. Pass out name cards for each child in your group. Have them print their first names on these cards.

◆ **Acting Justly.**   Have the children hold their books so that everyone can see one another's drawings and names. Invite each child to say his or her name, show the drawing, and tell about what they like to do for others. Have the group respond to each child with a big handclap.

◆ **Praying Together.**   After the children gather in the prayer center, help them to punch a hole at the top of the name card and attach string or yarn through the hole. You should have a name card for yourself. Hang your card first and say something, such as: "Dear God, I thank you for my own special name, _____ ." Ask each child to hang his or her name card on the "Naming Tree" and say similar words.

Now invite the children to hold hands around the prayer table. Light the candle as you explain that this will be a special place where we can talk and listen to God. Lead them in praying this prayer:

Catechist: Dear God, thank you for all the special children here today.
   Thank you, God, for (Janie).
   Dear God, please bless (Janie Wilson).

Children: God bless (Janie Wilson).

Lead the group in blessing each child until all in the circle have been blessed. Include yourself in the blessing prayer.

You are a catechist. God has called you by name to be here.

Our family names show who we belong to. We are not alone.

Day 2

◆ **Gathering Together.** Gather the children and direct their attention to the name cards on the Naming Tree. Since this is the beginning of the year, focus on the name of each child, one at a time, and have the rest of the group repeat the name.

◆ **Sharing Together.** Have everyone turn to pages 8 and 9. Read aloud the story to the end of page 8 and then ask, "How would you solve the story of the two Emilys?" Continue the sharing by asking, "Do you know anyone with the same name as yours?" If any children in your group respond, "Yes," invite them to share their feelings.

• Continue reading the story on page 9. Explain that we have a first name and a family name. Our first name tells who we are. Our family name tells what family we belong to. Help the children to print their family names in the space provided at the bottom of page 9.

When all have finished printing their family names, have the children sit in a circle holding their family names facing one another. Allow each child to share his or her family name. Congratulate each child on belonging to such a special family.

Distribute construction paper in the shape of a rectangle. Divide the children into pairs. Invite the partners to share with each other an activity they like to do with their families. Then have one partner draw on one side of the paper what he or she likes to do with family members. Then have the other partner do the same on the other side. Ask both to talk about what they can contribute to their families.

◆ **Acting Justly.** Let the children introduce their partners to the group and share what they have drawn and what they have learned about the families of their new friends. Then have the children add these pieces of paper to the Naming Tree.

• Learn the Theme Song. You may wish to teach the first verse of the Theme Song, "My Name," from the cassette *Songs for Living Waters 1.*

◆ **Praying Together.** Review some of the family names and family activities on the Naming Tree. Then gather the children in a circle around the prayer table, light the candle, and say, "Let us think about our families. (Pause) Our family names show us that we are not alone. (Pause) We share so many happy times with our families."

Explain that we are all going to pray now for each of our families. Go around the circle and ask each child to say his or her family name. After each response, use the following prayer:

Catechist: For the (Wilson) family, we thank you, God.

Children: We thank you, God, for the (Wilson) family!

Day 3

◆ **Gathering Together.** Mention to the children that today they will discover another special kind of name. Begin a dialogue about some common nicknames, such as Curly, Rusty, Blondie, Skip, Butch, or Princess. Point out that we call these special names nicknames.

◆ **Sharing Together.** Explain that when we meet together, we will call each other by name. Names are important to us. We should be careful about the names and nicknames we call one another. Just as we would not like to be called a mean name, we must not call anyone else by a name that is mean.

• Have the group turn now to page 10. Read the page slowly to the children to present the idea that some nicknames are short, others are long, and some tell something about a person. Ask whether the children in the story like their nicknames.

Next direct attention to the long, slim child on page 10. Roberto did not like his nickname until he rescued his dog, Dusty. Then the nickname took on a whole added meaning because Roberto, Slim, was now a hero. Roberto now liked his nickname because it stood for something wonderful. Explain to the children that no matter what the name, every child is unique and special. No matter what our nicknames may be, it is how we feel about ourselves that is important.

◆ **Acting Justly.** Distribute drawing paper and crayons and ask the children to draw a picture of a make-believe friend doing something good for someone else. Their picture should show their "friend" with one of the nicknames you have discussed. Encourage them to draw characteristics that would lead them to call their "friends" by these nicknames. Move around the room to compliment the children on their efforts and to ask whether they would also like to be called by the nickname.

After everyone has finished responding, bring the children into a circle to share their drawings. Let some volunteers show their drawings and explain what their friend is doing. Then allow other volunteers to share their drawings without any explanation. Let the group guess the nickname and give reasons for their choice.

• Sing the Theme Song. Sing the first verse of the Theme Song, "My Name," from the cassette *Songs for Living Waters 1.*

◆ **Praying Together.** Have the children bring their drawings to the prayer center. Give them time to think about the nickname given to their imaginary friend. Then invite everyone to repeat after you:

Catechist: Thank you, God, for each one of us. (Repeat)

Thank you, God, for all our names that tell who we are. (Repeat)

Do you know someone with the same first name as yours? How do you feel about sharing your name?

Have you ever had a nickname? How did you feel about it?

It is how we see ourselves that determines how we feel about a name.

Naming something shows that it belongs to us.

Day 4

◆ **Gathering Together.** The focus of this day will be to have the children realize that naming something shows that it belongs to us. Review the thoughts and ideas expressed about names during the past three days.

◆ **Sharing Together.** Now have the children talk about their favorite toys or pets. Invite them to tell whether they helped choose their pets' names or nicknames. Explain that sometimes when we give names to our pets or toys, the names show that they belong to us. Ask the children to mention some other things that they have named.

• Continue by asking such questions as "Can anyone else name what you own? Can you name what belongs to someone else? Why not? What are some things in this room that you can own by putting your name on them?" Examples might be the children's books, drawings, lunchboxes, clothing, book bags, and so on.

• Now direct the children's attention to all the fanciful toys and animals that border pages 10 and 11. Invite them to go around the border and name these pets and toys. Allow time for all the children to tell the reasons for their choices.

◆ **Acting Justly.** Bring in a stuffed animal and let the group have fun choosing a name for it. After everyone has had a say in offering suggestions, let the children decide what the name should be. Have the children discuss the kind of care the stuffed animal needs or live animals need.

As an optional activity, place a long sheet or individual sheets of large butcher paper on the floor. Let the children lie face-up on the paper as you trace around their outlines. Invite the children to print their first and family names at the top of the outlines and then decorate the insides of the outlines. Let them print and draw what they like to do, who they like to play with, what their family members do for one another. The outlines might be cut out and pasted around the room for all to see.

◆ **Praying Together.** Gather the children in a circle around the prayer table and have them hold hands. Begin the prayer celebration with the catechist introduction on page 12. Follow the directions given there.

You may wish to teach the hymn "We Are Walking in the Light" from the *Hymnal for Catholic Students,* #199.

THE NAME OF JESUS

God's Word

In ancient Israel, to change a name meant that the person had undergone a transformation and had become a new person.

In the Old Testament, to be named is to be known, to be summoned into presence. Is this different from the way we use our names?

Journeying in Faith

For the people of ancient Israel, names were more like our nicknames. Each had its own special meaning. They stressed the uniqueness of the person. Thus the name Abraham, deriving from a special event in Abraham's life, means "Father of many." Benjamin means "favorite son," and Joshua, from which the name Jesus was derived, means "God saves."

If anyone changed a name, the change had great significance. It meant that the person had undergone a transformation and had become a new person. So the change of name from Abram to Abraham and Jacob to Israel indicated significant experiences in their lives.

We also have significant experiences in our own lives. But we don't often change our name. Maybe we should change them to indicate a new person or a fresh start. What do you think?

The name of Israel's God, YHWH, was understood to be so powerful that it could not be uttered. To call on the name of YHWH was to invoke God's presence, to summon God to action. The divine name had all the power of YHWH. When Goliath approached David, he came with spear and javelin. David said to Goliath, "You come against me with sword and spear and scimitar, but I come against you in the name of the LORD of hosts" (1 Samuel 17:45).

In the Old Testament, to be named is to be known, to be summoned into presence. The name is the person. So the name of the Lord God was constantly praised:

> Praise, you servants of the Lord,
> praise the name of the Lord.
> Blessed be the name of the Lord
> both now and forever.
> From the rising to the setting of the sun
> is the name of the Lord to be praised.
> (Psalms 113:1–3)

This same understanding of name is in the Gospels. It is a theme of the story of Elizabeth and Zechariah. As Luke presents it, they were anxious for a child. Zechariah, while praying in the Temple, experiences God's presence. God's messenger tells him, "Your wife Elizabeth shall bear a son whom you shall name John" (Luke 1:13).

The name John (Hans, Juan, Jean, Ivan, Sean, Evan, Ian) means "God is gracious." For Elizabeth and Zechariah, God was good to give them this child, and they proclaimed this goodness by naming him John.

*The name John means
"God is gracious."
Do you know what your name
means?*

Christos *describes Jesus Christ's
life work. What name could
describe your life work?*

Jesus spoke often of the name of the Lord. He described his mission as having "made your name known to those you gave me out of the world" (John 17:6). The people asked him if he was the Messiah. He responded, "The works I did in my Father's name give witness in my favor" (John 10:25). He prayed, "Father, glorify your name" and, "O Father most holy, protect them with your name which you have given me" (John 12:28; 17:11). When he taught his disciples to pray, he taught them, "Our Father in heaven, hallowed be your name" (Matthew 6:9). When he entered Jerusalem, the people cried out, "Blessed is he who comes in the name of the Lord" (John 12:13).

This understanding of Jesus' name is reflected in the Gospels. In the story of the Annunciation, Luke portrays Mary at prayer. In prayer, she experiences God's presence. The presence is described as an angel sent from God. The angel tells Mary, "You shall conceive and bear a son and give him the name Jesus" (Luke 1:31). It is not Mary who names the child. It is God who does the naming.

Mark begins his gospel with the words, "Here begins the gospel of Jesus Christ" (Mark 1:1). Jesus' surname is not known. He is commonly named in the gospels as "Jesus of Nazareth." After the Resurrection, he was referred to as "Christ." It is something of a "throne name" indicating that he is King, Lord of heaven and earth. *Christos* is the Greek word which conveys something of the Hebrew word *Messiah,* the anointed one. It was common for kings to be anointed in ancient times. By their use of this name, the Christians professed that Jesus was God's anointed one, or the Messiah, "the one sent from God." This was the good news they proclaimed when they preached to people the Gospel of Jesus Christ.

PART TWO
THE NAME OF JESUS

God's Word

Journeying in Faith with Children

Aims

- To consider that families choose names with special meaning for their children
- To learn about Mary and Elizabeth
- To learn about the gospel story of the naming of John the Baptist
- To explore the gospel story of the naming of Jesus

New Words

Bible   Jesus   Christ
John   Savior

Materials

Day 1: • name cards: Mary, John, and Elizabeth

Day 2: • name card: John the Baptist
- construction paper
- crayons or markers

Day 3: • name cards: Mary, Jesus, and Savior
- duplicated sheets
- crayons

Day 4: • name card: Christ
- crayons or markers

Use *The First Christmas,* VHS (Credence Cassettes) on Day 3

Theme Song

"My Name" from the cassette *Songs for Living Waters 1* by Stephen Chapin

Day 1

◆ **Gathering Together.** Gather everyone together and ask them to sit in a circle. Have the children open their books to page 13. Have them notice that each group is a family. Let them talk about who is pictured in each family group. Some families are large; other families are small. Spend adequate time here so that the children understand that all families have people who love one another very much.

◆ **Sharing Together.** Read aloud the text on page 13 about how families choose names. Invite volunteers to share a story of their naming or the meanings of their names.

• Explain that today we are going to share some stories of people who have very special names. Carefully remove the Bible from its place in the prayer center. Explain that this book has a special name. We call it the Bible. Let everyone repeat the name after you. Continue to stress that the Bible has many wonderful stories about special people. Explain that they will learn some of these stories throughout the year.

• Read the story of Mary and Elizabeth from page 14. Hold up a name card as each person is introduced. The name card should have the name of Mary or Elizabeth or John on the front and the meaning of each name on the back. Let the group use the drawing on page 14 to retell the story. Ask for ideas about what Elizabeth and Mary might be saying.

◆ **Acting Justly.** Continue discussing the meaning of John's name, "God is good." Ask the children to name people or things in their lives that show God is good. Emphasize that the people who love and help us show us God is good. Invite volunteers to talk about ways they could show others that God is good.

◆ **Praying Together.** Gather the children in the prayer center. Have a child place the name cards for Elizabeth, Mary, and John on the Naming Tree. Offer a simple prayer celebration, for example:

Catechist: Thank you, God, for the wonderful stories from the Bible. Thank you, God, for giving us Elizabeth and Mary. Elizabeth chose such a good name for her baby, John.

Children: Thank you, God.

Catechist: We know that *John* means "God is good."

Everyone: Thank you, God. You are good!

John means "God is good."

John wanted to tell others to love God and one another. Where do you hear this message today?

Day 2

◆ **Gathering Together.** Begin by singing the first verse of the Theme Song, "My Name," learned in Part One. Review the story of Elizabeth naming her baby by asking such questions as "Who remembers the names of the people we talked about yesterday? Do you remember what the name *John* means? Why do think Elizabeth named her baby 'John'?" If the children have any difficulty in answering, let them look at the drawing on page 14 and retell the story.

◆ **Sharing Together.** Ask the children if they know of any people who have titles before their names, for example, Officer, Father, Doctor, Professor, and so on. Explain that a person is called by a title because it tells the kind of work she or he does. Talk about the title President, which we give to the leader of our country, or use other examples familiar to the children.

• Continue the story of John as it appears on page 15. Use a name card as done with the other names. Help the children to see that John wanted to tell others to love God and one another. As you help the children understand why John was known as the Baptist, explain that he baptized people with water when they promised to try again to love God and one another.

If time permits, you might all enjoy role-playing the story of John the Baptist. Show the children how John the Baptist poured water over people who were standing in the river. Explain that this is what happened at their own baptism.

◆ **Acting Justly.** Distribute construction paper to each child. Direct the children to make simple drawings that show what they know about John the Baptist. Their drawings may include Elizabeth and Mary with the baby John, John talking to a group of people, or John baptizing people with water as seen on page 15. Each child should include people's names at the bottom of his or her drawing. When all are finished, ask some of the children to tell the story of their drawings.

Then distribute one more page to each child. Invite the children to draw themselves doing something that shows they love God and one another. After volunteers have shared this final drawing, punch holes in the pages and tie them with yarn or staple them together. Encourage the children to actually do what they have just drawn.

◆ **Praying Together.** As the children gather for prayer invite a child to hang the "John the Baptist" card on the Naming Tree. Then lead the children in this prayer: "Let us remember how happy Elizabeth was to name her son 'John.' John told us to love God and one another. Let us open our eyes. We love God and one another!" Have the children answer, "We love God and one another! Amen."

Day 3

◆ **Gathering Together.** Begin by singing the first verse of the Theme Song, "My Name." Review the names *Elizabeth, Mary,* and *John* and the title of John as the Baptist. Tell the group that today they are going to talk about the most important name of all. It is the most important name because it belongs to the most important and loving person of all time.

◆ **Sharing Together.** Direct the children to open their books to pages 16 and 17. Use the name cards for Mary and Jesus to tell the story of Mary naming her baby "Jesus." Remind everyone that Mary was a cousin of Elizabeth and lived in a little town called Nazareth.

• Soon Mary had her baby, too. She named him "Jesus." She was so happy because the name *Jesus* means "God saves." Hold up the name card for Jesus. Mary knew that her son would save many people. Ask the children what *to save* means.

Explain that Jesus saves us by always loving us and showing us how to be happy. He saves us by giving us friends and family to help us. Ask for volunteers to talk about some of Jesus' friends who help them, for example, Mom and Dad, an older relative, or a neighbor.

◆ **Acting Justly.** Emphasize that Jesus saves us from being alone. That is why one of Jesus' names is "Savior." Explain to the children that no matter what happens in our lives, Jesus tells us that God is always with us. God loves us. Ask, "How can we show our love for God and others?"

Distribute to each child a copy of a sheet that has the name *Jesus* printed with dots and that you have prepared in advance. Have the children use crayons to connect the dots and then decorate the edges of the paper. Invite the children to take the drawings home. Ask them to remember to say "Jesus says God is always with us!" when they give the drawing to a loved one. You might print the message on the bottom of the sheet before duplicating. Emphasize that we know that God is always with us.

◆ **Praying Together.** As some children place the name cards for today on the Naming Tree, light the candle. Quietly explain to the children that because Jesus is so special in our lives, many people bow their heads when they hear or say the name *Jesus*. Bowing shows love and respect. Ask the children to follow along with you in prayer and bow their heads when they hear or say the name *Jesus* in the prayer.

Catechist: Jesus, your name means "God saves."
          You save us from being alone.
          You tell us that God is always with us.

Children: Jesus, we love you. Amen.

Jesus saves us from being alone. Jesus is our best friend. How does this make you feel?

Jesus tells us that God is always with us.

Day 4

◆ **Gathering Together.** Gather the children together and begin by singing the first verse of the Theme Song, "My Name." Review previous learning by asking such questions as "Who was Mary? What is the name she gave to her baby? What does the name *Jesus* mean? (God saves.) Why is *Savior* one of Jesus' names? (Jesus saves us from being alone.)"

◆ **Sharing Together.** Recall that Elizabeth's son, John, received a second name that was a title. Ask: What was John's title? Why was he called John the Baptist? Remind the children that we often give titles to people. For example, we call people Coach, Doctor, Judge, and so on. Titles are names that describe what people do. John told people that they should love God and one another. When they promised they would try, John baptized them with water.

• Have the children open their books to pages 16 and 17 as you explain that Jesus' friends called him "the Christ." Hold up the name card for Christ for all to see. *Christ* is a name, or title, given to Jesus because it describes Jesus' life.

Explain to the children that when Jesus grew up, he traveled about, telling people that God loved them. What a wonderful message to tell someone. Continue the story of Jesus and the meaning of his names as explained on page 17. Your tone of voice and manner will be most important here to show the joy in Jesus' message and name. Jesus' friends knew that he was the "One sent from God." He is the only person ever given this name or title. Jesus Christ is God's own Son.

◆ **Acting Justly.** Distribute crayons or markers and allow the children to color the name *Jesus Christ* on pages 16 and 17. After they have finished, ask them to name a way they can help people not feel alone.

◆ **Praying Together.** Have a child place the name card for Christ next to Jesus and Savior on the Naming Tree. Then gather everyone around the table in the prayer center. Conduct the prayer celebration as found on page 18. Remember to review these celebrations thoroughly before the lesson. These are a vital part of your catechesis.

You may wish to include the hymn learned in Part One, "We Are Walking in the Light" from the *Hymnal for Catholic Students,* #199.

In the name of Jesus, you are blessed.

Jesus is the Christ. How do you reverence his name?

MY NAME IS "CATHOLIC"

The Church

We are all brothers and sisters of one another for we are all sons and daughters of God. Are the people in your city or town "connected" to one another as in a family? Why or why not?

Jesus calls upon us to share this vision of our relatedness to all people. Do you feel connected to your brothers and sisters in the Christian family? Why or why not?

Journeying in Faith

By name, we are identified as unique persons. Within our family, we are set apart, individualized by name. Each person in the family has his or her own special name. If two persons in the family have the same name, then one of these persons is called by another name, a nickname, or a title.

We belong not only to a particular family, but also to the whole human family. We name this "God's family." God's family is made up of people of all races, nationalities, and creeds. All people are God's creatures. All belong to the human family. All people, men and women, girls and boys, the elderly and the young, the married and the single, the sick and the well, belong to the human family. All people from many different places and from different walks of life share in a common humanity. We are all brothers and sisters of one another for we are all sons and daughters of God.

That God loves and desires the salvation of all people is the good news that Jesus preached. He called his disciples to preach this same good news to all people. Jesus did not discriminate. He saw all people as God's people, all members of the human race united under God as our Father. He calls upon us to share this vision of our relatedness to all people.

Think of your city, town, or community. How would you describe the feeling of people about our connectedness as one human family? What problems exist? What opportunities are there for people to come together to help one another as family? And where do you stand in all of this?

We also belong to another family. This family, called Christian, is made up of all persons who believe in Christ. The members of this family share in the life of the Father, the Son, and the Holy Spirit. We share in divine life.

As Christians, we are brothers and sisters of Jesus, and through him, of one another. As sisters and brothers, we ought to help one another grow. We do this by sharing our life through generous acts, instruction, correction, love, and prayer for and with others.

The division of the Christian family into many churches is a scandal. Every Christian is in some way responsible for healing this division among Christians.

United with Christ, Christians are named the Church. The Greek word EKKLESIA, "church," was a name for a people called out. It was regarded in this sense long before the word was used to name the place of worship. Christians were called "the church" or "the assembly." Church is a name the New Testament gives first to any local assembly and then to the whole body of believers. It is a name given to us through entrance into the community at baptism. All members of the assembly are together the Church.

As Catholics, we share a common faith experience and understanding about the meaning of life with others who name themselves Catholic. How is the Catholic Church like a family to you?

As Christians, we belong to the Catholic Church. As our family name is Christian, so we could say our first name is Catholic. Although we do not want to overemphasize the difference among Christian churches, we recognize that differences exist. As Catholics, we share a common faith experience and understanding about the meaning of life with others who name themselves Catholic. If someone came to you and asked why you are a Catholic, what would you say? Why do you belong to the Catholic Church? How is the Catholic Church like family to you?

As Catholics, we celebrate our faith together in our liturgies. We profess our faith together in a creed that many other Christian churches also proclaim. We listen to God's word, which we call on the Church that we make up to help us interpret. We articulate our understanding of our faith in doctrinal teachings. We are united together as many churches in all parts of the world through the bishop of Rome, whom we name the Vicar of Christ. We are named the Roman Catholic Church.

The entire community of believers is the Catholic Church. In the past, this name has sometimes been used to refer to the bishops of the church or generally to the clergy. This is inadequate because it is an incomplete meaning of the word *church*. The Catholic Church is the entire community of the faithful. Unless we appropriate this name Catholic to ourselves, we do not appropriate all the rights and responsibilities that come with the name.

The names we accept express who we are and call us to become more fully what we proclaim to be. How does the name "Catholic" express who we are and who we are called to be?

To accept a name shared with others is to accept the life, the past, the present of that community. It is to accept its values, its meanings, its attitudes toward life. It is to accept a vision of life. Names give us identity and relate us to others. The names we accept express who we are and call us to become more fully what we proclaim to be.

My Name Is "Catholic"

Journeying in Faith with Children

The Church

Aims

- To think about all the children we know by name
- To understand that we are all God's children
- To know why we are called Christian
- To take joy in naming ourselves Catholic

New Words

Christian
Catholic
parish

Materials

Day 1: • none
Day 2: • cutout letters
  • crayons or markers
Day 3: • name card: Catholic Church
Day 4: • wallpaper roll
  • crayons, markers, and other creative materials

Theme Song

"My Name" from the cassette *Songs for Living Waters 1* by Stephen Chapin

Day 1

◆ **Gathering Together.** Begin by singing the first verse of the Theme Song, "My Name." Remind the children that all people have family names. Family names tell us to whom we are related. They show us that we have others who love and care for us, who help and protect us.

◆ **Sharing Together.** Direct the children to open their books to page 19. Have them finish the four faces by making them look like some children they know. Invite some to tell the names of the children whom they have drawn. Perhaps they know the meaning of their friends' names or why their friends were given their particular names.

• Invite the children to look at the charming drawings of children from around the world on pages 20 and 21. Have the group guess where some of these children live. Elicit comments on the various clothing worn by the children in the drawings. Point out that all the children in the drawings belong to one large family. People may dress differently and speak differently, but we are all members of God's family. Stress that we are all God's children.

• Have the group talk about the things children everywhere would like to have, for example, enough food to eat, a home, freedom, friends, a loving family, a place to play, happiness, and so on.

◆ **Acting Justly.** Inquire if the children think that brothers and sisters are always happy together. Encourage the children to be as specific as possible as they respond to the question: "What can we do to make our brothers and sisters in this room happy?" You may want to list the children's suggestions on the chalkboard or a wall chart. Extend the discussion to include your parish and the neighborhoods the children live in.

◆ **Praying Together.** Have children stand in a circle holding hands.

Catechist: God, you made us all. We all belong to one large family.

Children: We are all God's children. (Raise grasped hands)

Catechist: God made us all.

Children: We are all God's children. (Raise grasped hands)

Catechist: All of us are sisters and brothers in God's family.

Children: We are all God's children. Amen. (Raise grasped hands)

As followers of Jesus, we take on a new name, Christian. How does that make a difference in your life?

What makes a group of people Christian?

Day 2

◆ **Gathering Together.** After gathering the children, briefly review our relationship to others in our large family, God's family. Ask if any of the children have done an act of kindness for a member of our large family, God's family, today. If so, let volunteers share their acts of kindness with the rest of the group. Highlight how happy we feel when we show our love for all of God's family.

◆ **Sharing Together.** Remind the children of all the different ways we are named. We have a first name, a family name, and, possibly, a nickname. As you begin to explain page 21, stress that we all share another name.

• Take out large cutout letters that spell *Christian.* As you spread out the letters, ask why a family would be named Christian. Recall that the title *Christ* means "the One sent from God." Emphasize that Christ was a title that was given to Jesus.

Show that the title *Christ* is contained in the name *Christian.* We are called Christians because we are named after Jesus Christ. That means we try to live as Jesus. We love one another and we help one another. We all love Jesus very much.

• Help the children to learn the second verse of the Theme Song, "My Name."

◆ **Acting Justly.** Now let the group enjoy coloring the "I am a Christian" name sign on page 21. Try to elicit from the children how we can show we are Christians in other ways than wearing the name sign. Mention that when we help a friend in need, help our parents, or just give a friendly smile to someone, we are showing that we are followers of Jesus Christ. We call ourselves Christians.

◆ **Praying Together.** Close with the following prayer:

Catechist: Dear Jesus, we are all brothers and sisters in God's family.

Children: We are called Christian.

Catechist: We are named after Jesus Christ.

Children: We are called Christian.

Catechist: When we love one another,

Everyone: we are called Christian. Amen.

Day 3

◆ **Gathering Together.** Help the children to recall that we are all named Christian. We are all related to one another because we all belong to the Christian family. We are all named after Jesus Christ.

• Sing the first and second verses of the Theme Song, "My Name."

◆ **Sharing Together.** Explain that there are many families within the Christian family. Ask if any of the children can name another Christian church in your neighborhood. There may be a Methodist, Baptist, or Lutheran congregation in the area with which they are somewhat familiar. Some children in all likelihood will have a non-Catholic parent. When discussing this, be positive.

Introduce to the children that some of us in the Christian family have the name *Catholic.* We call ourselves Catholic. We belong to the Catholic Church. You may want to show a name card that says Catholic Church. You might then have the children add the card to the Naming Tree.

• Have the children turn to pages 22 and 23 in their books. Join in the fun as the children discover all the people and sights on these pages. Mention that all the people pictured are happy to call themselves Catholic. They all belong to the Catholic Church.

Draw the children's attention to the church building shown on page 22. Stress that sometimes we use the word *church* to describe a building, such as the one pictured on the page. But when we say that we belong to the Catholic Church, we mean we belong to all the people, including us, who are Catholic. We are the Catholic Church. Read the text on pages 22 and 23 and answer any of the children's questions.

◆ **Acting Justly.** Ask the children to name one simple way they could show others that they are Catholic, for example, helping a friend find a missing toy. Talk briefly about some of the acts of kindness that are done by the Catholic Church, for example, visiting the sick and elderly, collecting food and clothing for the homeless, and so on.

◆ **Praying Together.** Conclude with this simple prayer service:

Cathechist: God, we thank you for our Christian family.

Children: God, we thank you.

Catechist: God, we thank you for our Catholic family.

Everyone: God, we thank you for our Catholic family.
Amen.

We are all brothers and sisters because God made us all. We are one family. How does this make a difference to you?

What makes a group of people Catholic?

What makes your parish Catholic?

Day 4

◆ **Gathering Together.** As the children settle around you, ask them to name the church to which they all belong. Hopefully, they will shout happily, "The Catholic Church!" Emphasize that we all belong to the human family. Everyone we meet is our brother or sister. We are all children of God. However, we have other names by which we call ourselves. We are Christian. We are Catholic. We are so happy to be the Catholic Church.

• Sing the first two verses of the Theme Song, "My Name."

◆ **Sharing Together.** Explain that many, many people share the name *Catholic.* They live all over the world. They live in parishes. Each parish has a name. Ask the children to name the parish to which they belong. Print the name of the parish on the chalkboard for all to see.

Perhaps some children in your group have visited other parishes. Invite them to talk about what they saw and who they met. Share your own experiences of visiting other parishes in the area. Help the children to see that all these parishes, distant and local, are part of the Catholic family, the Catholic Church.

◆ **Acting Justly.** Help the children to share ways your parish shows that it is a Catholic parish. Your parish serves those in need, prays together, celebrates Mass, and so on. Let some children volunteer what they like best about their parish.

• Assist the group in making a mural similar to the drawing on pages 22 and 23. The mural would reflect the neighborhood of your parish. Each child could contribute a drawing to the mural that shows homes, schools, your parish church, people, trees, animals, and, of course, themselves. The mural paper might be a wallpaper roll so that it could wrap around your room to give a real feeling of community. The children should be encouraged to show themselves helping or being friendly to others.

The mural could then be displayed one Sunday in your parish church. This activity would take time, but it is well worth the effort. It gives the children a visual representation of being a member of your Catholic parish.

◆ **Praying Together.** As the children gather around the Bible in the prayer center, conduct the celebration on page 24. You may wish to include the hymn "We Are Walking in the Light" from the *Hymnal for Catholic Students.* As the children leave, tell them how happy you are that they are members of your parish family.

You may want to send a note home to the children's families, asking them to have the children bring photos of their baptisms for use in the next chapter.

THE DAY I WAS NAMED

We Pray

Why are baptisms special moments?

We are called by name at our baptism. We hear, " (Name) , the Christian community welcomes you with joy." What does this tell you about the community's acceptance of each individual?

Journeying in Faith

Think about the baptisms that you have attended. What made them such special moments?

A baptism is sometimes called a christening. The word *christening* is a good synonym for baptism. When christened, a person becomes a Christian and enters into and is accepted by the Christian family. The baptized becomes a member of the Body of Christ. Sharing in the life of the church, in Christ's life, the new Christian is initiated into a family that pledges to give support in living a Christian life.

The baptism of infants is the ritual moment for officially naming a child. In the past, Christians traditionally named their children after saints, men and women who were models of Christian life. That saint was called the "patron saint," one who would be an inspiration for the newly baptized.

Today, parents name their children for many reasons. Some still choose saints after whom they wish their children to model their lives. But for whatever reason a name is given, the name remains with the child to identify him or her throughout life.

The first question the priest asks parents at the baptism of infants is, "What name do you give, or have you given your child?" This question is asked for two reasons: first, so that the name may be given, and second, so that the child may be called by name throughout the baptism. The second question asked is, "What do you ask of God's Church for (name)?" It is at this point that the parents formally express the desire for the baptism of their child.

Throughout the ritual, the person being baptized is called by name. "(Name)," the celebrant says, "the Christian community welcomes you with joy." The entrance into the community is a very personal experience for the individual. The baptized is called by name to express the Church's acceptance of this particular individual into its community. It is this person, called by name, whom the community will support and care for. Listen carefully for these words at the next baptism you attend.

During the Baptism a short litany of the saints is said. By name, the great saints of the church are asked to pray for this candidate for baptism. Naming these saints recalls to all present the great Christian witness that they gave with their lives. The name of the patron saint of the parish, or other favorite saints, may be added to the litany.

The central and most significant prayer of the baptism is a naming prayer. Why do you think this is so?

The central and most significant prayer of the baptism is also a naming prayer. As the celebrant immerses the baptism candidate in the water, or pours the water three times over the person's forehead, he says, "(Name), I baptize you **in the name of** the Father, and of the Son, and of the Holy Spirit."

The candidate is baptized in the name of the Trinity. The Christian community is unique in believing in God as trinitarian. God, who created all that is, became incarnate in the one we name God's Son and dwells with the community through the Spirit. Men and women of many religions worship God, but only Christians believe in God as Trinity.

In baptism, this fundamental belief is expressed in the words by which baptism is celebrated. Christians are baptized in the name of the Trinity. The Creed, which Catholics say each Sunday as a profession of faith, is an expansion of this baptismal formula.

Christians believe in God, creator of all that is. They believe in Jesus Christ, who expressed in human life the love of God for all people. They believe in the Holy Spirit, whom Jesus called the Paraclete, who is the Giver of Life and with us now, strengthening and maintaining our union with one another and the Godhead.

Why is the Sign of the Cross a naming prayer?

Being baptized in the name of the Trinity gives a particular identity to the newly baptized. The person may now be named as Christian. He or she belongs to a community of those who believe in Christ and in the way of life he preached.

The Sign of the Cross is made in the name of the Holy Trinity. It is a naming prayer. It names us as a trinitarian people. It is a gesture we use throughout our lives. We name ourselves as believers in the triune God whenever we name ourselves with the Sign of the Cross.

What are your names?

We began this chapter by saying that our names identify us and relate us to others. What *are* your names? With whom do they relate you?

THE DAY I WAS NAMED

We Pray

Journeying in Faith with Children

Aims

- To appreciate how their families and the church celebrated their baptism
- To recognize that in baptism we are named members of God's family
- To learn the Sign of the Cross as a naming prayer

New Words

baptism
Sign of the Cross

Materials

Day 1: • name cards: Christian, Baptism

Day 2: • white and yellow construction paper
- glue, paste, or tape
- water
- card stock bases
- crayons, markers, and creative materials

Day 3: • bowl of water

Day 4: • white construction paper

Use *Baptism—We Belong to God's Family,* VHS (Don Bosco Multimedia) on all four days of this week

---

Theme Song

"My Name" from the cassette *Songs for Living Waters 1* by Stephen Chapin

---

Day 1

◆ **Gathering Together.** Ask the children if they celebrate their birthdays. Talk about their birthday parties. Explain that birthdays are special because they celebrate when we were born and how long we have lived. Everyone is happy to have us as part of the family.

◆ **Sharing Together.** Show them the pictures that you have of your own baptism or that of some child in your family. Share with them as much as possible about the baptism. When we are baptized, we become members of our Christian family. Show a name card with the word *baptism*. Invite volunteers to tell what they know about their baptisms. If some children have brought in photos, let them share along with you. Sometimes we call baptism a christening. When we christen someone, we make the person a member of the church community. As in baptism, we are named Christian. Show the card for Christian.

• Help the children to learn the last verse of the Theme Song, "My Name."

• Invite the group to open to page 25 in the child's book. Ask them to guess why the family in the picture is so happy. Encourage everyone to point to the new infant who is going to be baptized and become a Catholic Christian. Direct attention to the people of the parish pictured in the background. The entire parish family is always happy to welcome the newly baptized into the parish.

◆ **Acting Justly.** Remind the children that when we are baptized, we start a new life as a member of Jesus' family. We try to love Jesus and one another. That means we help one another. We try to live as a friend of Jesus. Ask for volunteers to describe one thing that they could do today to show that they are Christians, that they love Jesus and one another.

◆ **Praying Together.** Conduct this simple prayer service:

Catechist: Dear God, thank you for our baptism.
We are called Christian.

Children: We are called Christian.

Catechist: Dear God, thank you for all our families who help us to be Christian.

Everyone: We are called Christian. Amen.

23

Baptism brings us into the Christian family. We have Christian brothers and sisters all over the world.

Your parish church is a sacred place because the community gathers there to praise God. Do you experience God's presence there?

Day 2

◆ **Gathering Together.**   Today's session could take place in the church baptistry. Make sure that a baptismal candle, water in a font, and shell, or pourer, are available. A priest or pastoral associate may assist. If you hold today's session in your usual room, arrange the various items in the prayer center. As you gather the children together, sing all the verses of the Theme Song, "My Name." Review the previous session's discussion of baptism as a naming event in the life of a Christian.

◆ **Sharing Together.**   Lead the children through the meaning and actions of baptism as presented on pages 26 and 27 of the child's book. As you explain these pages, elicit questions and personal responses.

Describe how their parents thought deeply about what name to give to their precious new baby. The name that they chose meant they were happy and thankful to have a child in their lives. Always emphasize the good feelings associated with baptism.

Continue by explaining that their parents loved them so much that they brought them to their parish to be baptized. Friends, relatives, and parish members gathered to celebrate this event and to welcome them into our Catholic Christian family.

As you present page 27, you may wish to use a baby doll and actually pour water out of a shell or small pitcher. Make sure that everyone sees what you are doing. Demonstrate how the priest immerses the children in water or pours water over their heads at baptism. Review the words the priest uses.

◆ **Acting Justly.**   Emphasize that we are all baptized in the name of God. If we treat others as children of God, we can truly say we belong to the family of God. Have the children suggest something they will do to treat others as the children of God.

• Have the children make their own baptismal candles to take home. Distribute 5″ x 8″ pieces of white construction paper for the children to decorate. Then help them roll the paper into the form of a candle. Glue or tape it together. Add a small flame from a 2″ x 2″ square of yellow paper cut in half. Tape or paste the flame inside the candle. Mount the candles by gluing them to squares of heavy, white construction paper on which the children have printed their baptismal names.

◆ **Praying Together.**   If you are in the church baptistry, gather around the baptismal font for the prayer. Focus the prayer on remembering that we are all baptized and thanking God for being God's children. Adapt the prayer to whatever setting you are in.

Day 3

◆ **Gathering Together.** Begin by singing all the verses of the Theme Song, "My Name." Recall the baptismal words and actions that the children experienced previously. If the children went to the church baptistry, invite volunteers to tell the group what they remember the most about their visit.

◆ **Sharing Together.** Remind the children that when the priest used water at their baptism, he said, "I baptize you in the name of the Father, and of the Son, and of the Holy Spirit." Emphasize that we become part of God's family because we are named God's children.

• Now demonstrate the motions to the Sign of the Cross as you say the words. Ask if any children know how to say the prayer. Most will have seen it done at Mass. The Sign of the Cross is our prayer for naming God.

Explain that we begin and end many prayers with the Sign of the Cross. Have everyone turn to pages 28 and 29. Let them enjoy the drawing of the child making each step of the prayer.

Demonstrate the steps of the Sign of the Cross first. Then do it together as a group. Be sure that the children start with their right hand and that they follow the numbers. Move among the children as they begin to do each of the numbered actions. Be sure to face the same direction as the children. Once they have done the words and motions correctly, you might want to have them break into pairs to practice what they have learned.

Be sure that the children understand each action as pictured. Help them do the actions in correct, successive order and say the appropriate words that accompany the action. The knowledge of the children will vary. Some may already know the prayer. Others will be less certain. Let those who know the prayer help whoever is having difficulty. All the children should be congratulated on their learning the prayer.

◆ **Acting Justly.** If some of the children have helped a classmate to learn the Sign of the Cross, they are showing how much they care for others. Point this out to both partners. Emphasize that we feel happy when we help someone to learn and grow. Mention your own good feelings when you are together with the children. You help them to learn and develop. And they help you to grow as a person and as a catechist.

◆ **Praying Together.** Have a bowl of holy water available, if possible, so that the children may take turns prayerfully blessing themselves and making the Sign of the Cross. Gather around the Naming Tree. Call each child by name and invite that child to slowly approach the bowl of water and bless himself or herself.

Be an example of someone who prays with reverence.

Pray the Sign of the Cross thoughtfully.

How has baptism changed your life?

Day 4

◆ **Gathering Together.** Begin by singing all the verses of the Theme Song, "My Name." Conclude this first chapter of *Living Waters 1* by summarizing its main points. Begin by again showing photos of your own baptism. If you have children of your own, show pictures of their baptism, too. Emphasize that at baptism we are named as Christians and welcomed into the Catholic Christian family.

◆ **Sharing Together.** Invite each child who has brought in pictures of her or his baptism to show them and tell about them.

• On white construction paper prepare for each child an outline of the type of pitcher or shell used in your parish for baptism. Have the children draw in the water and decorate the paper with smiling faces, a happy scene, or bright colors. On the reverse side, help them to print their individual names and the words "Thank You!" These can be given to loved ones at home as a thank-you for having the children baptized. Have the children bring their completed shells to the prayer corner. Arrange them under and around the Naming Tree.

How does your baptism call you to change the lives of others?

◆ **Acting Justly.** Explain to the children that through their baptism they were asked to live like Jesus. For example, you might say, "In baptism you were asked to be good to others, to forgive them when they hurt you, and to help them when they are in need." Invite the children to suggest several ways they can do this.

• Present pages 31 and 32 as a simple method of reviewing the major themes of the chapter. These "Remembering" pages are easy to understand and serve as a clear summary of the preceding lessons.

◆ **Praying Together.** The prayer celebration on page 30 can be a simple, but profoundly moving, service. Follow the annotations for the prayer.

You may wish to include the hymn learned for Part One, "We Are Walking in the Light" from the *Hymnal for Catholic Students,* #199.

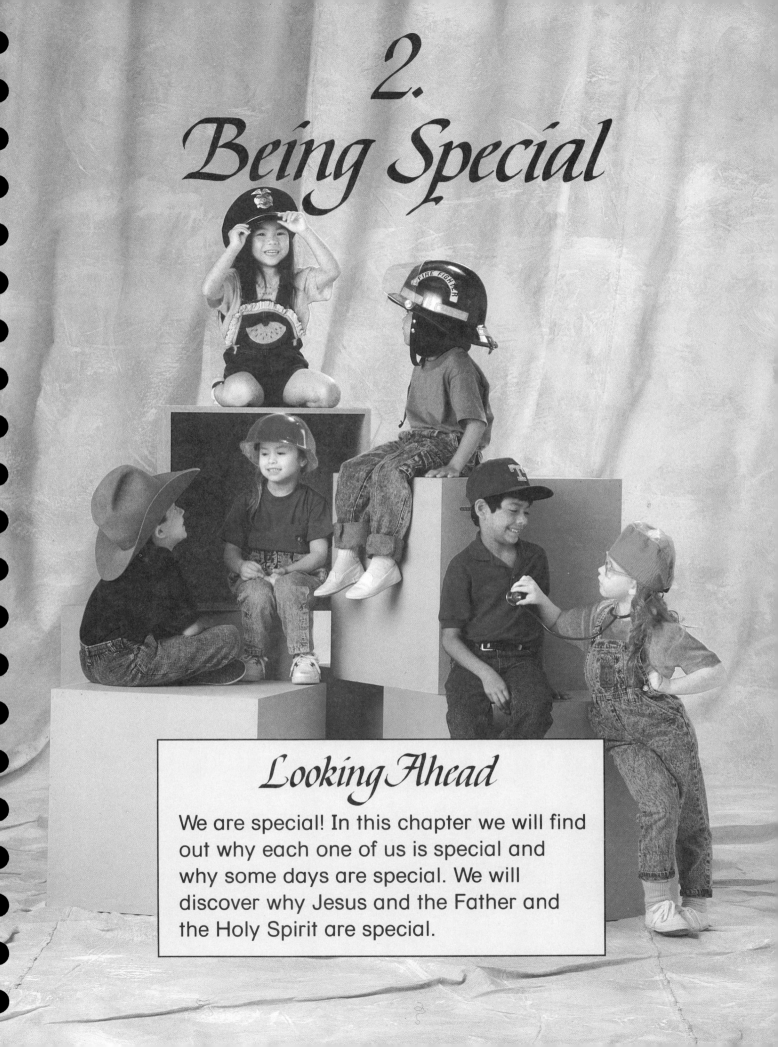

2.
Being Special

Looking Ahead

We are special! In this chapter we will find out why each one of us is special and why some days are special. We will discover why Jesus and the Father and the Holy Spirit are special.

Chapter Aims

OUR LIVES

To grow in awareness of special people and special times in our lives

GOD'S WORD

To learn from the Bible about people considered special by Jesus and become aware of those who treated him as special

THE CHURCH

To come to appreciate the special relationship of Jesus to God the Father and to the Holy Spirit; to become aware of how we show our love to others as Jesus did

WE PRAY

To learn that Sunday is a special day, the Lord's Day. To learn the gospel response and begin to learn the Our Father.

Chapter Two Theme Song

"Special" from the cassette *Songs for Living Waters 1* by Stephen Chapin

Using the Chapter Title Page

Invite the children to look with you at the picture on page 33, the Title Page of Chapter Two. Ask if they can identify each of the special hats worn by the children. The person who wears the hat in real life has a special job or role. Ask the children to describe the actions of each of these special people.

Read the chapter title to the children and then preview the chapter by reading the "Looking Ahead" box to the group.

Chapter Plan Ahead

Make arrangements for the following items well in advance of the session in which it is used.

• Order and preview the suggested audiovisual material. (Parts 2 and 4)

Audiovisual References

Learning About Jesus, VHS, St. Paul Books and Media, 50 St. Paul Avenue, Boston, MA 02130 (Part 2)

My Father's House, VHS, Franciscan Communications, 1229 South Santee St., Los Angeles, CA 90015–2566 (Part 4)

Music for the Prayer Services

"Happy the People" from the *Hymnal for Catholic Students,* #59.

"Alleluia!" from the *Hymnal for Catholic Students,* #39 or #75.

SPECIAL PEOPLE, SPECIAL TIMES

Our Lives

Who were the people who most influenced you when you were growing up?

Significant others shape what we do and think. How do they do this?

Journeying in Faith

If we can recapture our feelings and remember how we behaved the first time we fell deeply in love, we know what it means to meet a "significant other." Someone special entered our life. We wanted his or her approval and tried to avoid things of which the person would disapprove. This special person influenced the color of the clothes we wore, the kinds of recreation we planned, the company we kept.

Significant others shape what we do and think. Sometimes they influence us by what they say. But more often, they make themselves felt in our lives in more subtle ways, such as with frowns or smiles, with silence or merriment. We want to please, and in wanting to please the persons we love, we are transformed into someone they can love in return.

For many years the *Reader's Digest* ran a series, "The Most Unforgettable Character I've Ever Met." Without judging who the "most" unforgettable one is, we can all list people who made a great impact on us at one stage or another in our life. There was mother and dad. We may have taken them for granted. It was only in later years that we came to appreciate the degree to which they made us who we are.

For some, a grandparent is that most influential person. A young boy or girl may remember a retired school teacher who seemed to know everything and had almost as many books as the public library. Adults are often able to think back to a specific teacher who greatly influenced their thinking.

At one time, it seemed that the special people who attracted us wore uniforms: the starched white of a nurse, the brown and white habit of a nun, the tailored blue uniform of a state trooper, the yellow hard-hat of a construction worker. They were our heroes. They were what we wanted to be when we grew up. At a later age, our heroes may have been the public figures of entertainment and sports.

In growing up, we filled our world with these special people. As youngsters, we identified with them in a variety of emotional ways—from the deep love for a parent to a childhood crush on a junior high school teacher. It was not so much what they said or did as how they related to us. Because of the fascination they held for us, we tended to give their words more weight, their advice greater importance. In subtle but lasting ways, we took on the roles and attitudes of the significant others in our lives.

Are there times in your adult life that you find yourself imitating some special person? How does that make you feel?

Ultimately, we adopted their values, what was important in terms of success, and their ideals, those hopes and standards of perfection. A young girl's self-image reflects the expectations of both men and women in her life as to how she should act and the career she should pursue. A young boy becomes "male" in responding to the expectations of the adult world in which he finds himself.

Take the time, right now, to think of someone who was such an influence in your life as a young child. Visualize a specific moment with that person. Who was he or she? Why was that person so important to you? Are there times in your adult life that you find yourself imitating this special person? How does that make you feel?

Psychology and sociology confirmed what sensitive parents and gifted teachers have known from the beginning. Effective education rests on imitation. Everyone, but young people in particular, absorbs the values and ideals from adults whom they find attractive in their daily lives. Imitation is of crucial importance in the moral growth and social development of impressionable youth.

Who are the people in your life whose values you have absorbed?

Organized societies attempt to broaden the horizon of children beyond the immediate family by promoting formal education. In school, they come into contact with adults who have other concerns and talk about different things than their parents. The teachers themselves present other models. The men and women who people their books of fiction, history, and current events broaden their choices.

The school presents other possibilities, but it seldom makes as deep an impression as the adults one meets in his or her own earliest years at home. Nonetheless, it is important to understand how adults impact on the world of children. We influence the kind of adults they will become, just as the significant others of our childhood and adolescence helped us make us who we are.

PART ONE
SPECIAL PEOPLE, SPECIAL TIMES

Journeying in Faith with Children

Our Lives

Aims

- To identify special people, what makes them special, and how they affect our lives
- To identify special times, what makes them special, and how they affect our lives
- To realize and appreciate our own specialness

New Words

special

holiday

Materials

Day 1: • photo of someone who is special to you
- drawing paper, pencils, and crayons
Day 2: • quiet background music
Day 3: • crayons
Day 4: • construction paper, scissors, crayons
- candle

Theme Song

"Special" from the cassette *Songs for Living Waters 1* by Stephen Chapin

Day 1

◆ **Gathering Together.** Gather the children around the chalkboard. Have the word *special* printed in very large letters on the chalkboard. Ask the children if they recognize the word or can tell the group its meaning. Explain that today they will be talking about special people in their lives. Point out that each of us may have different people who are special to us.

◆ **Sharing Together.** Show the children a photo of someone who has played an important part in your own life. Explain to the children why this person is so special. Tell how this person has helped you.

• Give each child a sheet of drawing paper and pencils or crayons and invite each of them to draw a picture of a special person. As the children draw, walk around the room and enjoy their pictures. When all the children have completed their drawings, invite them to come up and show their pictures to the group. Collect the drawings at the end of today's session for use on Days 2 and 4.

• Invite the children to open their books to page 35. Give them a few moments to study the pictures. Then have them respond to the first two questions on page 35.

• Teach the first verse of the Theme Song, "Special."

◆ **Acting Justly.** Read a story to the children that illustrates a special person in a child's life. For example, "My Grandson Lew" tells of the many loving things Lew remembers about his grandfather. Talk about ways that the children can show how grateful they are to those who have played an important part in their lives. The children can show their gratefulness by telling others about the special people in their lives, doing a kind act for them, writing a note to thank them, and so on. Encourage the children to do one of these things for the special person whose picture they drew.

◆ **Praying Together.** Ask the children to assemble quietly in the prayer center and to bring their drawings with them. Begin by making the Sign of the Cross with reverence. Invite each one by name to show his or her drawing. After each child finishes, the group should say, "Thank you, God, for special people." End with the Sign of the Cross.

Who is special in your life? What makes a person special?

There are people special to the children, people who influence their young lives. What people have changed your life?

Day 2

◆ **Gathering Together.** Begin by singing the first verse of the Theme Song, "Special." Distribute the pictures of special persons that the children drew the previous day. Ask the children to sit in a circle around you and to bring their pictures with them. Invite the children to stand one at a time and show their drawings once again to the group and name their special persons. Recall with the children some of the qualities that make these people special.

◆ **Sharing Together.** When all are finished, collect the drawings. Ask the children to sit quietly and listen as you read a story about a little girl named Lian. Encourage them to picture in their minds each scene as you read it. Ask them to listen carefully for the names of all the special people in the story who helped to find Lian. Then read the story on pages 36 and 37 with great feeling. Use gestures whenever possible.

• When the story is finished, have the children open their books to the story on pages 36 and 37 and examine the pictures. Call on several children to tell what they think is happening in each picture. Ask the children to name all the special people who helped to find Lian. Talk about how each one helped.

• Point out to the children that it is important to look around and notice all the wonderful people who help us in so many ways each day. These might be a parent, librarian, mail carrier, or dentist. Then invite the children to suggest the names of other special people. Talk about what each one does for us that makes them so special.

◆ **Acting Justly.** Invite each of the children to tell which special person they would like to be like when they grow up. Encourage them to give a reason for their choice.

Invite the children to think about how he or she can be like that special person. Then allow volunteers to act out something before the group that their person does for them. Have the group guess what is being acted out. Talk about how these things will help the children to become better persons. Encourage them to talk to their special people about what they admire about them.

◆ **Praying Together.** Gather the children in the prayer center. Have some quiet, prayerful music playing in the background. Ask the children to bow their heads. Encourage them to think about the people who are special to them. Then pray slowly, "Thank you, God, for all the special people you have brought into my life. Help me to be like the people who are special to me. We pray in Jesus' name. Amen."

Day 3

◆ **Gathering Together.**   Begin by singing the first verse of the Theme Song, "Special." Gather the children together and invite them to open their books to page 38. Give them a few moments to look quietly at the pictures.

◆ **Sharing Together.**   Read together the first two sentences on the page. Invite the children to name their favorite holidays and to tell why they like them best. Share your own favorite holiday.

• Talk about the pictures on page 38. Ask the children to tell what is happening in each picture and why the people in the pictures are celebrating. Help the children to see that there is one day, our birthday, that is special to each of us.

Identify the child in your group whose birthday will be coming up next and the one who last celebrated his or her birthday. Explain that we celebrate our birthdays to share our joy over the gift of life, which we all received from God. On our birthday, each one of us has a chance to remember how special we are.

• Have the children look at page 39 in their books. Read the page and have them answer the questions. Give each child an opportunity to take part. When the children talk about receiving gifts on their birthdays, help them to see that the giving of birthday gifts is a special way for people to say how happy they are that God has given the gift of life to someone.

• Invite each child to decorate the picture of the birthday cake on page 39 of their books. Be sure that each one puts on the cake the number of candles that will tell his or her age.

◆ **Acting Justly.**   Help the children to understand that one way that they can show how grateful they are for a gift is by using it well. For example, you might ask how a child who receives a bicycle, an electronic game, or a doll might use that gift to show how he or she is grateful. Go on to explain that we can show God how grateful we are for the gift of our lives by being kind to others, being friends with someone who is lonely, sharing what we have with those who have less, and so on.

◆ **Praying Together.**   Have the children form a circle around the table. Ask them to think quietly about the wonderful gift of life God has given them and about how special each one of them is. Ask them to think of one thing that they will promise to do this week to show God that they are grateful and that they want to become even more special. Call each child by name. Invite each child to share what he or she will do.

Do you have a special holiday? Why is it so special for you?

Are your birthdays special celebrations for you? Why or why not?

What do you admire most about children?

We thank God always for the special people in our lives. For whom do you give thanks to God?

Day 4

◆ **Gathering Together.**   Begin by singing the first verse of the Theme Song, "Special." Ask each child to find the drawing of his or her special person mounted on the wall. Have the children, one at a time, walk to their drawing, point to it, and say, "My special person is _____." Have them take their drawing down and return to their seat with it.

◆ **Sharing Together.**   After each child has returned to his or her seat, walk around and place your hands on the head of each child. Say each child's name and state one thing about the child that is special. You might say, "You have a beautiful smile" or "You always try to help others."

• Give each child a strip of construction paper about 4″ wide by 20″ long and a pair scissors. Have the children cut the paper in the shape of a crown. Give them crayons to decorate the crowns. They should print their names on the front. You may wish to have a pattern for them to follow or you might want to cut out the crowns in advance.

Talk with the children again about how special they are. Recall how on our birthday we all celebrate the wonderful gift of life God has given us. Have each child wear his or her crown. Sing with them an appropriate song about being special or have them recite the following, using the suggested gestures:

> I am special. (Pointing toward themselves)
> Don't you see? (Pointing toward their eyes)
> My name is _____. (Pointing toward themselves)
> And God made me. (Hands uplifted)

◆ **Acting Justly.**   Have the children look again at the drawings they have made of special people in their lives. Have each child say once again what the person does that makes him or her so special. Try to draw out the ways these people are kind and helpful. Help the children to see how we all can be kind and helpful to others.

◆ **Praying Together.**   Gather the children in the prayer center. Light a candle on a table in the center. Ask the children to close their eyes for a few moments and to try to be very quiet inside themselves. Then begin by reverently making the Sign of the Cross. Together celebrate the prayer on page 40 of their books. See annotations.

Let the children keep their crowns on during the prayer service and have them bring and hold up the drawings of their special persons. The children should take home their crowns and drawings.

You may wish to teach the hymn "Happy the People" from the *Hymnal for Catholic Students,* #59.

God's Word

What is it about Jesus that attracts you the most?

How did Jesus change the lives of the people of his times? How has he changed your life?

PART TWO
JESUS IS SPECIAL

Journeying in Faith

We sometimes hear it said that an individual has a "magnetic personality." The phrase describes a person who attracts people the way a magnet draws metal to itself. Jesus of Nazareth was such an individual. According to the gospel accounts, he attracted many people to himself.

The magnetism of Jesus drew people from all walks of life. There were working men like the Zebedee brothers, James and John, who were fishermen. There were religiously earnest types like Simon the Zealot. There were Pharisees like Nicodemus, a leader in the Jewish community who came to Jesus at night (John 3:1–5). Among Jesus' followers, there were several women of means who used to provide for Jesus and his disciples. These women included Mary Magdalene, Johanna, the wife of Herod's steward, and Susanna (Luke 8:2–3). Jesus was a family friend of Martha and Mary and their brother, Lazarus, whom he visited from time to time (Luke 10:38–42).

All who opened themselves to Jesus found that he changed their lives. Simon, later called Peter by Jesus, is one of the heroes of the New Testament. Once Peter's brother, Andrew, introduced him to Jesus, Peter abandoned his boat and nets and went fishing instead for people (Mark 1:16–17). Peter belonged to that inner circle of disciples who shared Jesus' most intimate secrets. Peter was among the first to confess Jesus to be the Messiah. (Matthew 16:16). But it was also Peter who tried to persuade Jesus to follow a safer path and avoid crucifixion (Mark 8:32).

Despite the fact that Peter said he would lay down his life for Jesus, in a moment of weakness, he denied knowing him. Peter wept bitterly for this lapse of faith. In the end, it was Peter who rallied the disciples after Jesus' death (Acts 1:15–22) and became a leader in keeping his memory alive. Once Jesus had become the "significant other" for Peter, it changed the disciple's values, attitudes, and ideals.

Jesus was special also to a man named Zaccheus. Zaccheus, a rich man, lived in Jericho. Many people avoided Zaccheus because of his reputation as a tax collector. In order to get a good look at Jesus, he climbed a tree. When Jesus saw him, he said, "Zaccheus, be quick and come down. I must come and stay with you today" (Luke 19:5). Some criticized Jesus for going to the house of a sinner. Zaccheus, for his part, was so attracted to Jesus that he promised to reform his life. "Here and now," he said, "I give half my possessions to charity; and if I have cheated anyone, I am ready to repay him four times over" (Luke 19:7–8).

35

The children found Jesus to be special and were drawn to him as a friend. Can you imagine why?

Does Jesus make a difference in your daily life? How?

Children also found Jesus attractive. Parents brought them to see him. Despite the objections of his disciples, Jesus welcomed them. He put his arms around them, laid his hands upon them, and blessed them. He instructed his disciples, "Let the children come to me; do not try to stop them; for the kingdom of God belongs to such as these" (Mark 10:13–16).

Human himself, Jesus understood children and held them up as examples of what it means to have simple faith. Things hidden from the wise and sophisticated are known to children because of their simplicity (Matthew 11:25). Children instinctively acknowledge their dependence on others and are not too proud to ask for what they need (Matthew 18:4). Jesus was protective of children, knowing how impressionable they are (Matthew 18:6). It is no wonder that many children found Jesus to be special and were drawn to him as a friend.

The Samaritan woman at the well is another person whose life was changed by Jesus (John 4:4–42). Tired and worn out by his traveling, Jesus sat down near Jacob's well while his disciples went to town to get some food. As the Samaritan woman approached the well, he asked her for a drink of water. "Recall," says John, "the Jews have nothing to do with Samaritans" (John 4:9). And Jewish men had even less to do with Samaritans who were women.

Jesus spoke to the woman. He told her of God's love for her and for all people, Jew and non-Jew alike. Upon returning to the well, his disciples were shocked that he was holding a conversation with a woman. The woman, however, recognized Jesus as a prophet and accepted his claim to be Messiah. She responded to him with faith and then left to call others to come and listen to him. Her life had been changed by this meeting with Jesus.

Make some time during today to simply think of the life and the person who is Jesus. Like the woman at the well, your life will be changed in big and small ways by him.

PART TWO
JESUS IS SPECIAL

God's Word

Journeying in Faith with Children

Aims

- To introduce Jesus as our very special person
- To show how Zaccheus' life was changed after meeting Jesus
- To familiarize the children with the story of Jesus' kindness to the woman at the well
- To help the children recognize Jesus' special love for them and for all children
- To recall Jesus' special love for us and for all people
- To celebrate Jesus' special love for children

New Word

Zaccheus

Materials

Day 1: • Bible
        • name card: Zaccheus
Day 2: • construction paper hearts
        • Bible, music
Day 3: • none
Day 4: • Bible, candle

Theme Song

"Special" from the cassette *Songs for Living Waters 1* by Stephen Chapin

Day 1

◆ **Gathering Together.** Gather the children around you in a circle. Begin by singing the first verse of the Theme Song, "Special." Then ask the children to close their eyes for a moment and picture in their minds someone who is special to them. Invite volunteers to tell about their special persons. You may wish to model this by telling a story about someone who is special to you.

Have the children open their books to page 41. Ask and share responses to the three questions that focus on special people in our lives. Be sensitive to various family situations as you listen to responses to the questions.

Give the children time to examine the pictures on the page, and have them tell why each person depicted is so special.

• Reverently hold up a Bible and ask if they know the name of this special book. Show them the word *Bible* in the book or write it on the chalkboard. Explain that the Bible is a wonderful book that has many stories about God in it. Ask them to find the first sentence on page 41 about the Bible and to read it together aloud.

◆ **Sharing Together.** Have the children read the last sentence on the page. Talk with them about Jesus' great love for them and for all people. Ask them to listen carefully as you read them a story about how Jesus showed this love.

• Show a card with Zaccheus' name on it. Read the story on page 42 slowly and dramatically. Have the children listen to discover why Jesus was a special person for Zaccheus. After the reading, discuss why Jesus was a special person to Zaccheus.

◆ **Acting Justly.** Have the children read the last two sentences on page 42. Talk about ways they can be honest. Explain that if we always try to be honest, Jesus will help us because he is our special friend.

◆ **Praying Together.** Have the children stand in a circle and join hands. Pray, "Jesus, you are our special friend. The Bible tells us that you love us all. You teach us how to be honest and how to love one another. Amen."

Jesus is special to all of us. How is Jesus special for you?

Always remember how much Jesus loves you.

Day 2

◆ **Gathering Together.** Bring the children together in a circle with a Bible placed on a table in the center. Sing the first verse and teach the second verse of the Theme Song, "Special." Recall what they learned the day before about Zaccheus. Tell the children that today they will hear another story from the Bible and point out that the story tells us how Jesus became someone else's special person.

• Ask the children to look at the illustration on page 43 in their books as you read them the story of the woman at the well. Explain what a well is. Explain how people in Jesus' time got their water from a well each day.

◆ **Sharing Together.** Read the introduction to the story on page 43. Have the children listen to discover why Jesus was special to the woman. Invite the children to add details to the story as you go along by asking such questions as "What do you think the woman was thinking? What else do you think Jesus might have said to her?"

At the end of the reading, ask the children to indicate why Jesus was a special person to the woman at the well. Discuss how wonderful it must have been for this woman who was so lonely to find out that Jesus loved her and was her friend. Explain that Jesus loves us in this special way and is our friend, too. He wanted the woman and all of us to know how much God loves us.

• Give the children time to examine and comment on the picture of the woman at the well talking with Jesus on page 43. You may wish to include all the children in a dramatization by letting one play Jesus, one play the woman, and all the rest of your group play the people in her town. Encourage the children to be as spontaneous as possible.

◆ **Acting Justly.** Give each child a heart cut out of construction paper with the word *lonely* printed on it. Talk about how lonely the woman at the well felt before she met Jesus. Have the children cross out the word and add another word that will tell how the woman felt after she met Jesus. Talk with them about how Jesus wants us to help people who are lonely to be happy. Discuss ways the children can do this. Then turn the hearts over and have them draw what they will do.

◆ **Praying Together.** Gather the children in the prayer corner in front of the table on which the Bible has been placed. Begin with the Sign of the Cross. Have some quiet music playing in the background. Invite each child to come and place his or her paper heart on the table and say, "Jesus, help me to be a good friend to someone who is lonely." Have the group respond "Amen" after each child's prayer. End with the Sign of the Cross.

Day 3

◆ **Gathering Together.** Gather the children in the sharing center. Sing the first two verses of the Theme Song, "Special."

Have the children open their books to pages 44 and 45. Tell them that you would like to read them a story about a time when lots of people crowded around Jesus. Ask them to listen carefully to see how Jesus reacted. Have them listen as well to discover how children are special to Jesus.

Read dramatically the story of Jesus and the children. Use gestures while telling the story. For example, you might stretch out your hands out invitingly as you say, "Let the little children come to Me!" Lay your hands on each child's head in blessing as you relate how Jesus blessed the children.

◆ **Sharing Together.** Have the children look at the picture on pages 44 and 45 as you read. Ask them how they can tell from the picture that Jesus loves the children. Talk with them about how these children who were so close to Jesus must have felt.

Ask the children in your group how Jesus shows his love for them today. Point out that Jesus cares for them through their families.

◆ **Acting Justly.** Ask the children to read the last two sentences on page 44. Talk about some ways they can love others as Jesus did. For example, they might help someone who is tired, be friendly to someone who is lonely, invite a new child in the neighborhood to join in their games, and so on. Use pictures to illustrate these and other ways.

◆ **Praying Together.** Gather in the prayer corner. Ask softly, "How does it feel to know that Jesus loves you in a special way? What would you like to say to Jesus?" Invite the children to tell him quietly in their own hearts how they feel, and how much they love him. Give the children a few moments to pray quietly. Then end with this prayer, "Jesus, thank you for loving us in a special way. We love you, too. You are our special friend. Help us to be loving as you are." Have all the children respond with "Amen."

Those who opened themselves to Jesus found their lives changed. Has this happened to you?

Jesus spoke to the woman of God's love for her and for all people. Jesus changed her life.

Day 4

Christians have a responsibility to respond to the needs of the ill, hurt, or lonely. How will you help?

◆ **Gathering Together.** Gather the children and sing the first two verses of the Theme Song, "Special." Ask the children to close their eyes and sit quietly for a few moments as they think about all the people they learned about this week. Invite them to recall the stories of Zaccheus, the woman at the well, and Jesus and the children.

◆ **Sharing Together.** Have the children open their books to page 45. Read the first three sentences together. Review the stories of Zaccheus, the woman at the well, and the children by asking the following questions: "How was Jesus a special person to Zaccheus?" "How did Jesus show God's love?" "What did Jesus do to show Zaccheus how to be kind to all people?" Use similar questions for the stories of the woman at the well and Jesus with the children. Then help the children apply the stories to their own lives.

◆ **Acting Justly.** Have two children dramatize the scenario presented on page 45. Talk about other ways they can be kind, especially to persons whom others do not like. Some examples might be inviting these people to play with them, talking with them during recess, helping them with homework, sharing with them at lunchtime, inviting them to their home, and so on.

What needs of the children are you responding to?

◆ **Praying Together.** Gather the children in the prayer center. Place a Bible on the table and a lighted candle next to it. Before beginning the prayer, appoint a child to carry the Bible reverently to you after you announce the reading.

Ask a second child to carry the lighted candle and to accompany the bearer of the Bible. Have the candle bearer stand next to you as you read slowly and with feeling the story of Jesus and the children. You may wish to read the account from Matthew 19:13–15 or Luke 18:15–17. If you prefer, have a copy of the story from the child's book taped to the inside of the Bible for the reading. When the reading is completed, have the candle bearer lead you back to the table.

Then, move to each child and lay your hand on each one's head as you say, " (Name) , Jesus loves you. You are special." Have the children respond "Amen" after each blessing. Follow the annotations for the remainder of the prayer service.

You may wish to include the hymn "Happy the People" from the *Hymnal for Catholic Students,* #59.

THE FATHER AND THE HOLY SPIRIT ARE SPECIAL

The Church

God, the creator of the universe, is involved in our lives like a loving parent. How can we respond to such great love?

Fatherhood suggests care and protection, guidance and love. What other images of God help you know of God's love for you?

Journeying in Faith

Although it is impossible to understand how God can be at once Father, Son, and Spirit, the images suggested by these three titles give us rich insights into the mystery, beauty, and power of God. It is because God is revealed in Jesus as Son that we know God also as Father and Spirit.

Some people never know their father. Some dislike their fathers. But everyone has an image of what an ideal father is, or at least should be. Father (and this is true of mother as well) is not a name. Rather it expresses a relationship. It speaks of a person responsible for our being. It tells us of our origins or roots. Others may know our fathers as mechanics, salesmen, doctors, supervisors, government employees, or whatever. But children often have a special relationship with their fathers that life-long friends and even wives do not.

Fatherhood suggests care and protection, guidance and love. It commands respect, evokes appreciation. It is a familiar relationship, which is to say, that it is intimate and affectionate and spontaneous. In our culture, fathers seldom stand on formality. It is common for children, young and old, to call their fathers "DAD," "DADDY," or some similar name of endearment.

Jesus taught us to call God our Father. It is a special revelation. God, the creator of the universe, the sun, stars, earth, and living beings, is also involved in our lives like a loving and concerned parent! When we think about it, the enormity of this reality staggers the imagination. But think about the impact of this revelation on Jesus' audience. The ancient Jews saw God as an awesome force who required respect and reverence. They were not permitted to even utter God's name. Then Jesus appears on the scene and tells them to address God as "ABBA," a term of endearment. He opened a whole new dimension of God's being.

There is no limit to God's goodness, and God expects us to be equally generous in dealing with one another. Like a loving parent, our heavenly Father is concerned for the good and bad alike. Jesus said:

But now I tell you: love your enemies and pray for those who persecute you, so that you may become the children of your Father in heaven. For he makes his sun to shine on good and bad people alike, and gives rain to those who do good and to those who do evil. Why should God reward you if you love only the people who love you? Even the tax collectors do that! And if you speak only to your friends, have you done anything out of the ordinary? Even the pagans do that! You must be perfect—just as your Father in heaven is perfect. (Matthew 5:44–48)

The Spirit is free and freeing: it liberates us from our worse selves, from sin and from fear. What image of the Holy Spirit is most powerful for you?

Just as caring parents sense the needs of their children, Jesus assures us that our heavenly Father knows our needs before we ask. We pray simply as Jesus taught us, addressing Our Father in heaven who is close to us on earth. We ask for present needs while hoping for the coming of God's kingdom. We plead for forgiveness in the measure that we forgive those who wrong us. And finally, we pray that God keeps us out of harm's way.

God is Father. God is also Spirit. We could not properly be called children of God were it not for the Holy Spirit. It is the Spirit who enables us to cry, "Abba, Father" (Romans 8:15).

How do you talk about the Spirit of God? On Pentecost, the disciples experienced the force of the Spirit. Bewildered by the events subsequent to Jesus' death, they were gathered together "when suddenly there came from the sky a noise like that of a strong driving wind, which filled the whole house where they were sitting. There appeared to them tongues like flames of fire, dispersed among them and resting on each one. And they were all filled with the Holy Spirit." (Acts 2:2–4)

What do you pray to the Spirit to be freed from?

The Spirit is power, the force of wind. The Spirit is fire who inflames passionate commitment and enthusiastic zeal. The Spirit is the light of truth and wisdom. The Holy Spirit manifests the power of God, the giver of life. Like the wind, the Spirit blows where it will. The Spirit is free and freeing: it liberates us from our worse selves, from sin and from fear. The Spirit comforts and encourages in moments of sadness and despair. The Spirit speaks unity, thus healing division. The Spirit sanctifies: it makes us whole, the beginning of holiness. The Spirit extends a fresh beginning: it renews the face of the earth.

Think about significant past experiences in your life. Recall the movement of the Spirit in those experiences. Have you had similar experiences recently?

PART THREE
THE FATHER AND THE HOLY SPIRIT ARE SPECIAL

The Church

Journeying in Faith with Children

Aims

- To consider how we like to be like people who are special to us
- To learn about God the Father and the Holy Spirit
- To begin to learn the Our Father
- To understand how the Father and the Holy Spirit are special to Jesus and to us

New Words

Abba
Our Father
Holy Spirit

Materials

Day 1: • drawing paper, tags
     • Bible
Day 2: • none
Day 3: • thin sheet of paper
     • candle
Day 4: • drawing paper, crayons
     • Bible

Theme Song

"Special" from the cassette *Songs for Living Waters 1* by Stephen Chapin

Day 1

◆ **Gathering Together.** Begin by singing the first two verses of the Theme Song, "Special." Have the children open their books to page 47. Give them time to examine the picture on the page. Then read slowly the first two sentences and have the children respond to the questions that follow. Invite them to imagine what the girl is thinking as she looks in the mirror. Ask who they would like to be like.

◆ **Sharing Together.** Examine the picture of Jesus on page 48. Remind the children that Jesus is special to all of us.

• Tell the children that Jesus had someone who was very special to him. Jesus talked about this special person very often. Jesus spoke often to the people about God whom he called his Father in heaven. Ask the children what they think Jesus might be saying to his Father.

• Ask volunteers to share how they address their fathers: Daddy, Dad, Poppa, Pop, and so on. Be sensitive to the fact that some children may have had an unpleasant experience of fathers. Explain that Jesus had a special name for his Father, too. He called him "Abba." This was a very loving way of saying Father. Read the material on page 48.

• Talk with the children about all the wonderful things God created. Explain that each thing is like a special gift of love from the Father. Give each child a sheet of drawing paper shaped like a gift box with a tag on it that reads: With love from God, your Father. Ask them to draw a picture of one of their favorite things that God made for them.

◆ **Acting Justly.** Hold up the Bible again. Tell the children that whenever Jesus talked about his Father, he always did it with great love. Encourage the children to talk to the Father in prayer. Talk about ways they can do this.

◆ **Praying Together.** As a closing prayer, have the children sing the following lyrics very slowly to the tune of "Frère Jacques":

> Abba, Father, Abba, Father,
> You are great, you are good.
> Jesus calls you Abba.
> We will call you Father.
> We love you. We love you.

43

(Our Father gestures)

Our Father who art in heaven,

hallowed be thy name. . . .
Give us this day our daily bread

and forgive us our trespasses, as we
forgive those who trespass against us.

And lead us not into temptation,
but deliver us from evil.

Amen.

Day 2

◆ **Gathering Together.** Begin by singing the first two verses of the Theme Song, "Special." Tell the children that Jesus often would take time out from his busy day to talk to God his Father in prayer. His followers would sometimes watch him quietly.

One day the apostles came to Jesus to ask if he would teach them how to pray. Make the story descriptive by suggesting that Jesus may have been sitting on a rock or on the top of a hill. Perhaps it was early evening and everyone was tired after a long day of work. Talk about the feelings of the apostles and how happy they must have been to be with Jesus. Jesus, too, must have been both pleased to have this time with them and happy that the apostles wanted to talk to God his Father, whom he loved so dearly.

◆ **Sharing Together.** Introduce page 49 in the child's book by pointing out that Jesus often talked to God his Father in prayer. Then have the children begin to learn the parts of the Our Father. Take each part of the prayer, and explain in simple terms the meaning of Jesus' words.

• Ask the children if they can remember a time when our parish family says this prayer together. Tell them that we all pray the Our Father at Mass. Point out that because this prayer is so special, we say it together each time we celebrate the Mass. Explain that the priest reminds us at Mass that Jesus taught us this prayer.

Be sure to come back to the Our Father each week and review the phrases that have already been learned. Then add a new phrase and gesture until the children have learned the entire prayer.

◆ **Acting Justly.** Have the children find the name of the prayer at the bottom of page 49. Read the question at the bottom of the page. Have them respond "Yes" together. Encourage them to ask people at home to help them learn the prayer.

Remind them that when they say this prayer, they are talking to the Father, who is very special to us. Encourage them to pray with attention and love, as Jesus did. Point out that when we pray the Our Father, we need to be forgiving of people who have hurt us.

◆ **Praying Together.** Gather in the prayer center. Invite the children to stand in a semicircle around the table. Tell them, "We are going to join Jesus as he says this prayer to his Father." Lead them in praying the Our Father slowly and with great reverence.

Day 3

◆ **Gathering Together.** Begin by singing the first two verses of the Theme Song, "Special." Show the children a picture of a relative or friend who has moved away. Tell them who the person is, how you first came to know her or him, and why this person moved away. Point out that because you and this person really care for each other, you are together in spirit even though there are many miles between you. Ask if any of the children has had a similar experience.

◆ **Sharing Together.** Ask, "When we care for and love special people, do we always have to be with them to remember them or feel close to them?" and "What are some ways we can be with people even though they are not right here with us?"

• Explain that Jesus knew that he would not always be with his followers. Because he loved them so much, he did not want them to feel alone. Jesus told them that he would send someone to be with them always. When Jesus talked about this person, the apostles could tell by the look of love in his eyes that it was someone very special to Jesus, as the Father was special to him. This special person was the Holy Spirit.

• Have the children read Jesus' words on page 50. Ask them to find the three sentences that begin with the words "The Holy Spirit . . ." Tell them that these sentences tell us three very important things we want to remember about the Holy Spirit. Read the beginning of each sentence and have them complete the sentence together.

• Invite them to examine the pictures on pages 50 and 51, one by one. Then invite the children to tell how the people in the pictures are showing love and care for others. Explain that the Holy Spirit helps people show care and love.

• Hold up a thin sheet of paper and blow on it gently. Ask the children what happens when you do this. Ask if they saw the breath that made the paper move. Explain that this can remind us of the Holy Spirit because even though we cannot see the Holy Spirit, we can tell the Holy Spirit is in our hearts by the way we act toward one another.

◆ **Acting Justly.** Have the children look at page 51 in their books. Read the first sentence and talk about what the sentence means. Do the same with each of the three sentences. Then have the children mark the pictures in the book that show children being kind and loving. Invite them to tell a story about each of the pictures they marked. Ask them how they can act in a kind and loving way.

◆ **Praying Together.** Place a lighted candle in the middle of a table. Invite the children to stand around it. Invite them to close their eyes and speak quietly to the Holy Spirit in their own words. Then have them open their eyes and lead them in praying together: "Thank you, Jesus, for giving us your Holy Spirit."

The Holy Spirit helps people to show care and love. Do you have a favorite prayer to the Holy Spirit?

When are you aware of the actions of the Holy Spirit in your life?

The Holy Spirit lives in our hearts and helps us to love God and one another.

Day 4

◆ **Gathering Together.**   Begin by singing the first two verses of the Theme Song, "Special." Gather the children and ask them to think about three special people that they learned about this week. Write on the chalkboard the names of the people the children identify.

◆ **Sharing Together.**   Recall with the children that the first person the group learned about this week is someone we know very well. The Bible tells us many stories about his life. He is our special person. He taught us by his life to be kind and loving to others. Ask if anyone can name this person. Print the name of Jesus on the chalkboard after a child gives the response.

• Talk to the children about God the Father. Tell them that God is special. Jesus called God "Abba." Jesus said that pleasing God was the most important thing in his life. Jesus wants us to please this special someone, too. Ask, "Who is this someone special?" Talk about why God the Father is special to Jesus.

• Repeat the same procedure for the Holy Spirit. Ask, "Who helps us to be kind and loving?" and "Whom did Jesus send to us?" Tell the children that Jesus promised to send this special one to his apostles and to us. Invite responses to the question, "Who lives in our hearts and helps us to love God and one another?"

◆ **Acting Justly.**   Give each child a sheet of drawing paper and crayons. Suggest that the children draw a picture of something that they can do to thank the Father, the Son, and the Holy Spirit for their love and care. When finished, have the children share their drawings with the group.

◆ **Praying Together.**   Gather in the prayer center. Invite the children to bring their drawings with them. Celebrate together the prayer on page 52. If the children have learned a melody for the Our Father, let them sing it. After the words "Give us your gift of kindness," have each child place his or her drawing on the table in front of a Bible. End with the suggested blessing.

You may wish to include the hymn "Happy the People" from the *Hymnal for Catholic Students,* #59.

SUNDAY IS OUR SPECIAL DAY

We Pray

*How do you make Sunday
a special day?*

*Sunday calls to mind the
resurrection of Jesus. How is it
celebrated as a special day in the
Church?*

Journeying in Faith

Sunday is different from other days. It is the day for picnics, family reunions, and parties. For most of us, it is a day when we relax our usual work schedule, restore our energies, and get ready for the week ahead. Sunday is for playing, reading, and sharing. It is the day of heavy newspapers, football, and afternoon naps.

Sunday is unlike other days. Everywhere that Christianity has made an impact, Sunday is a special day. But it was not always so special.

The word *Sunday* is a relic of the pre-Christian calendar used by the ancient Greeks. For them, it had no special meaning. It was simply the first day of the week. They named the days of the week after the planets: Sunday is the day of the Sun; Monday, the day of the moon; and Saturday, the day of Saturn. In some European languages, Spanish for example, the days in the middle of the week are named after other planets: *martes* or Tuesday (Mars), *miercoles* or Wednesday (Mercury), *jueves* or Thursday (Jupiter), and *viernes* or Friday (Venus). In Spanish, however, as in French and Italian, Sunday is called the "day of the Lord"—*domingo, dimanche, domenica.*

From the beginning, Christians considered Sunday to be special because it was the day of the resurrection of Christ. All the Evangelists note in their accounts of the resurrection that Sunday is the day of the resurrection. The first day of the week thus marks a new beginning.

The resurrection of Jesus changed everything for the early Christians. It is the event that inspired Christian faith. The resurrection of Jesus altered their whole vision of life. It was the mighty deed of God, to be celebrated in life and in worship. As the first day of the week was recognized as resurrection day, so it became the day of Christian worship, "the Lord's Day."

Every Sunday, the church celebrates the Eucharist. Sunday is the day on which the Christian community gathers to listen to the word of God and share the bread and wine. At the eucharist, we remember the passion, resurrection, and glory of the Lord Jesus Christ.

The Second Vatican Council noted that Sunday is "the original feast," and that other feasts of saints, such as the Blessed Virgin, unless they be of exceptional importance, shall not have precedence over Sunday. Sunday "is the foundation and kernel of the whole liturgical year."

Sunday is the foundation of the liturgical year. Why is this true?

In the early days of the Church, Christian writers went to great pains to make it clear that Sunday had nothing to do with the Jewish sabbath. In the course of time, however, they became associated in the popular mind. In A.D. 321, Constantine declared Sunday a holiday. He made an exception, however, for farmers lest the provisions of harvest or heaven be lost. The leisure time was intended to permit Christians to reflect on the new covenant that God had made with all people in Christ.

In our own time, Pope John XXIII has encouraged Sunday rest. He said that "it is right and necessary for people to cease for a time from labor, not merely to relax their body from daily hard work, and to refresh themselves with decent recreation, but also to foster family unity."

Sunday is special because it is the day when we proclaim the holiness of *every* day. Of course, God does not love us only on Sunday. But Sunday, resurrection day, the Lord's Day, is the day when we acknowledge the unchanging and continuing love of God that we experience every day.

What would the week be like without a Sunday?

Sunday is the day when we remember the service we are asked to offer others every day. It is the day when we stop and reconcile ourselves with any brother or sister from whom we have been estranged. Every day is a holy day, but Sunday is *the* holy day for Christians. It is the day of rest on which we pause and remember who we are and what God has done for us. On Sunday, we are reborn.

What would the week be like without a Sunday? What if every day was the same as every other day? No time for change, no time for rest, no time for relaxing, no time for games or festivity. If God had not given us Sunday, we would have had to create such a day ourselves.

How do we foster unity in our family on Sunday? in our parish?

Much of our society has forgotten the roots of its Sunday joy. It still shares in its benefits. It still needs its favors. But it is those of us who rejoice on Sunday, in our lives of sharing with Christ and one another, who truly can sing "Alleluia" and "Praise to you, Lord Jesus Christ!" This is the day which the Lord has made. Let us be glad and rejoice in it.

SUNDAY IS OUR SPECIAL DAY

We Pray

Journeying in Faith with Children

Aims

- To discover that Sunday is special
- To learn that Sunday is the Lord's Day
- To explore ways in which we keep Sunday special
- To learn the gospel response

New Words

Lord's Day	Eucharist
Mass	lectionary
Alleluia	Gospel

Materials

Day 1: • name cards: Sunday, Mass, Eucharist
- crayons or markers

Day 2: • name card: Alleluia, Alleluia, Alleluia,
- crayons or markers

Day 3: • picture of people at Mass
- drawing paper
- crayons or markers

Day 4: • lectionary
- candle

Theme Song

"Special" from the cassette *Songs for Living Waters 1* by Stephen Chapin

Day 1

◆ **Gathering Together.** Call on volunteers to name each day of the week. Ask the children which day of the week is their favorite day and why. Then tell them that today they will be learning about a day that is very special for all Christians. Name the days of the week very slowly, beginning with Monday, and ask the children to raise their hands when you mention this special day. Show the name card with the word *Sunday* on it.

◆ **Sharing Together.** Invite the children to offer reasons for Sunday being a special day. Ask what things they like to do on Sunday. Then have the children look at the picture on page 53 and share ideas about what the people are doing.

• Explain to the children that Sunday is a special day for those who believe that Jesus is special. Sunday is the Lord's Day. Read to them the text on page 54. Show a name card with the word *Mass* on it. Invite the children to share their experiences of going to Mass.

Show a name card for the word *Eucharist* or print the word *Eucharist* on the chalkboard. Have the children repeat it several times. Explain that it means "to give thanks." At Mass, we give thanks to God for all God's kindness.

• Follow the directions on page 54. Have the children draw their families coming to Mass on Sunday. Ask for volunteers to show and tell about what they have drawn. Be sensitive to the range of experiences the children have had in attending Mass with their families.

◆ **Acting Justly.** Point out to the children that there may be some Catholic children in the neighborhood who do not have the chance to go to Mass on Sunday. Suggest that the children talk with their parents about inviting another child to go to Mass with them on Sunday.

• Teach the third verse of the Theme Song, "Special."

◆ **Praying Together.** Gather the children in a circle and pray: "Thank you, Lord, for giving us Sunday as our special day."

What do you do to make Sunday a special day?

At Mass, we give thanks to God for all God's kindness. We thank God for letting Jesus be with us always.

Day 2

◆ **Gathering Together.** Gather the children in a circle and lead them in the song "If You're Happy and You Know It, Clap Your Hands." Invite the children to make up other verses that express ways of showing happiness; for example, "show a smile," "shout hooray," "raise both hands," and so on.

◆ **Sharing Together.** Describe the following incidents and have the children respond by clapping and shouting "Hooray!"

> You wake up in the morning and there is a blizzard outside. You hear the news on TV: "No school today!"

> The school is having a frog jumping contest. Your brother's frog is in the lead. Another frog is right behind. Your brother's frog makes a big leap and wins.

Tell the children that they are now going to learn a new word that means "We Praise God." Point out that the word is similar to the word *hooray.* Show a name card with the words *Alleluia, Alleluia, Alleluia.* Then have the children turn to page 55 in their books and see if they can find the words there. Read the page to them and have them decorate the Alleluia banner. As they are decorating it, encourage them to listen for this word when they are at Mass.

• Explain that the prayer they have just learned is used to introduce the reading of the gospel at Mass. Explain that the gospel reading is from God's holy book, the Bible. Remind the children that the Bible tells us about God's love and all the wonderful things Jesus did for us. Read together the first paragraph on page 56.

• Share with the children other examples of people who bring us good news. Examples might include a mother telling her family they are going to have a new baby, a child showing his or her parents a good report card, a mail carrier bringing a birthday or holiday card, and so on. Ask the children how they respond to good news. Explain that we have a special response to God's good news read to us in the gospel. Read the rest of page 56 with the children.

◆ **Acting Justly.** Suggest that the children listen very carefully to the gospel reading on the coming Sunday and that they share it with someone who may not have had the opportunity to go to Mass that day. For example, they might share it with a sick relative.

◆ **Praying Together.** Ask the children to think quietly about something special for which they would like to thank God. Call on each child to name one thing and to use the following words: "Alleluia! Alleluia! Alleluia! I thank you, God, for _____." After each child offers her or his prayer, have the group respond, "Amen, Alleluia."

Day 3

◆ **Gathering Together.** Tie a string around your finger and ask the children why they think you have done this. Point out to them that people tie a string around their finger to remind them of something that they do not want to forget. The string is saying, "Remember!" or "Don't forget!"

◆ **Sharing Together.** Have the children think about some of the important things Jesus taught that they have learned. These are things about which he might say, "Remember!" or "Don't forget!" Allow time for the children to reflect and offer responses.

• Show a picture of people at Mass. Explain that when we get ready to leave Mass, the priest reminds us, "Go in peace to love and serve the Lord." Ask, "How do we love and serve the Lord?" Invite the children to give examples of how they can do this.

Have the children turn to page 57 in their books. Have them listen as you read the page except for the last sentence. Then dramatize this part of the Mass, pretending you are the priest. Have them say the response together.

• Sing all three verses of the Theme Song, "Special."

◆ **Acting Justly.** Have the children reflect on what they have learned about loving and serving others. Then ask them to think of one way they might do this in the coming week. Pass out drawing paper and crayons or markers and have them draw one picture to illustrate what they will do. Have the children share their drawings.

◆ **Praying Together.** Gather in the prayer center. Invite the children to come forward one at a time and place their drawings on the table, saying: "Jesus, this is how I will love and serve you."

God wants us to carry into the week the word we hear at Mass on Sunday.

How do you "go in peace to love and serve the Lord"?

Sunday is a day to tell Jesus how glad we are that he is with us always.

Day 4

◆ **Gathering Together.** Begin by singing all three verses of the Theme Song, "Special." Write the words *Alleluia, Gospel,* and *Our Father* on the chalkboard and call the children's attention to them. Ask questions about the meanings of these words and recall what they have learned about them.

◆ **Sharing Together.** If possible, take the children to the church and show them the altar and the ambo, or lectern, and relate these to what the children have learned about the Mass.

Show the children the lectionary. Explain that the lectionary contains the readings we hear at Mass. Prepare to read a gospel. Invite the children to stand and sing Alleluia. After reading the gospel, say, "This is the gospel of the Lord." Then invite the children to respond, "Praise to you, Lord Jesus Christ." It is not necessary to go into great detail about the Mass. The children will learn more about this at a later time.

◆ **Acting Justly.** Talk with the children about the final words the priest says at Mass. Share that these words send us to love and serve the Lord as Jesus did. Ask them to think about what they will do today to love God and to show concern for others.

Use pages 59 and 60 as a review of the children's learning. Be sure to emphasize the connection between all sessions in the chapter.

◆ **Praying Together.** You may wish to have the children remain in church to celebrate the prayer service on page 58 of their books. If you celebrate the prayer in the classroom, place a lighted candle on a table in the center of the group as a reminder that Jesus is present with us.

You may wish to include the hymn "Happy the People" from the *Hymnal for Catholic Students,* #59.

3.
Hands Are for Helping

Looking Ahead

Little hands! Big hands! Helping hands! In this chapter we will find out how people use their hands to help others. We will learn what Jesus did to show us how to help people with our hands.

Chapter Aims

Our Lives

To discover and appreciate the work of our hands

God's Word

To learn from the Bible the ways Jesus helped others with his hands; to understand and appreciate the meaning of the Good Samaritan story

The Church

To hear stories of people who helped others with their hands, particularly St. Francis and St. Louise de Marillac; to decide how to help others with our own hands.

We Pray

To discover ways we can pray with our hands, especially at Mass

---

Chapter Three Theme Song

"Helping Hands" from the cassette *Songs for Living Waters 1* by Stephen Chapin

---

Using the Chapter Title Page

Invite the children to look at the picture on page 61, the Title Page of Chapter Three. Have them examine each of the three pairs of children. Ask how one of the children in each pair is using his or her hands to help the other person. Ask the children if they use their hands to help others in similar ways.

Read the chapter title to the children and then preview the chapter by reading the "Looking Ahead" box.

Chapter Plan Ahead

Make arrangements for the following items well in advance of the session in which they are used.

- Try to locate some stringed instruments or a horn of some type in order to demonstrate the sounds of musical instruments. Arrange to have someone actually play these instruments for the children. (Part 2)

- Read more about the life of St. Francis and St. Louise de Marillac. Biographies of both saints may be found in *The Catholic Encyclopedia,* which can be found in most public libraries. (Part 3)

- Find a book on signing and practice several signs for "Hello, I am so glad you are here," "I love you very much," and the like. Also try to obtain a book in braille. (Part 4)

Music for the Prayer Services

"Lord, Hear Our Prayer" from the *Hymnal for Catholic Students,* #40.

"Jesus, Jesus" from the *Hymnal for Catholic Students,* #140.

USING OUR HANDS

Our Lives

Think about your own hands. What do you express with your hands?

How many ways do you use your hands in a day?

Journeying in Faith

Did you ever break a bone so that your hand was in a cast? When a member of your family had a broken arm or a totally bandaged hand, did you notice how helpless the individual became? One loses the use of a hand and everything quickly becomes a major chore. Washing is an inconvenience. Dressing, especially the tying of bows and fastening of buttons, becomes difficult. A simple skill like eating becomes a clumsy exercise. Playing a musical instrument is all but impossible.

We suddenly appreciate the hundreds of things we do with our hands. We use our hands in making a living. We cook. We sew. We dial or push telephone numbers. We drive. We write. Most of our hobbies involve the use of hands. We use our hands to communicate. We assist one another in a variety of ways with our hands. We use our hands to keep our balance when we walk. Our hands give a "personal touch" to everything we do or make.

We speak of "skilled" labor. It is defined in terms of deftness or dexterity in the use of one's hands. A skilled worker is a person who has better than average ability to use his or her hands in such areas as woodworking, typing, and needlepointing. An artist's performance depends on manual skills involved in playing a piano or clarinet, painting a picture, engraving a piece of silver, carving a statue, and so on. A surgeon and a watchmaker need "good" hands. In sports, our success depends on the way we grip a golf club, tennis racket, or baseball. Of course, a magician's career is founded on the slogan, "the hand is quicker than the eye."

Professional actors speak with their hands as well as with their voices. They know the importance of gestures, just as dancers do who practice hand movements along with the movement of their feet. Traffic police use their hands like symphony conductors to give directions and bring some order into chaos.

A handshake says many things. As a greeting to a new acquaintance or an old friend, it speaks acceptance. After a dispute and in contractual matters, it is seen to pledge agreement. Husbands and wives are said to give their hands in marriage, a sign of their willingness to give to and accept from one another. We raise our right hand calling on God to be our witness when we take an oath.

The hand-clasp used by many African-Americans and other closely knit groups is a way of acknowledging the tight bonds which they share and their pledge to support and watch out for each other. We show respect by saluting the flag, just as soldiers and their officers salute one another for the same reason.

Hands are for lending and for helping. What are some of your favorite things to do with your hands?

While most of us are seldom conscious of it, physically challenged persons readily appreciate the potential that hands have as a means of communication. By the method of "signing," hearing-impaired people suggest ideas with gestures and spell with their fingers. Blind persons read braille, making the sense of touch substitute for the sense of sight.

We do not properly appreciate the sense of touch, probably because we too rarely reflect on it. It may be that it seems strange to talk about the ways we are affected by the soft and the hard, the smooth and the rough. A soothing touch from a caring parent or a loving spouse relieves pain and heals the heart. The firm fingers of a nurse or physical therapist relax sore muscles and taut nerves. In moments of fear and uncertainty, we reassure one another by clasping hands or gripping the arm of a dentist's chair.

"To extend a helping hand" is a way of saying that we help others in need. We instinctively reach out to help a person who has fallen or to pull a child back from danger. We prop a pillow under the head of a sick person, feed a baby, comfort the distraught. We lend a hand when a neighbor has a task that is too great for one person. We lend a hand to a family when we help repair a house or respond to an emergency. Hands are for lending and for helping.

Take the time to quickly jot down some of your favorite things that you do with your hands.

Now look at what you wrote. Do these words help to tell you and others who you are? What do they tell you about yourself?

USING OUR HANDS

Journeying in Faith with Children

Our Lives

Aims

- To recall the many ways hands can be used
- To decide how to give a helping hand to others
- To notice how unique our hands are

New Words

helping hand

Materials

Day 1: • none
Day 2: • crayons or markers
  • fingerpaint, sponge, and paper (optional)
Day 3: • construction paper
  • scissors
  • crayons or pencils
Day 4: • objects of various textures
  • paste or glue
  • pictures of helping hands
  • drawing paper
  • crayons or markers
  • construction paper
  • lectionary

Theme Song

"Helping Hands" from the cassette *Songs for Living Waters 1* by Stephen Chapin

Day 1

◆ **Gathering Together.** Gather the group around a table to look at one another's hands. Ask the children to name some things that we do with our hands. Call for responses and list some of the things we do: eat, paint, hug, work, dress, carry, pull, fingerpaint.

◆ **Sharing Together.** Now gather the children into a circle so that everyone can see one another's hands. Ask the children to hold their hands way out front. Elicit the differences that they see in one another's hands. For example, they may be various sizes or colors. Emphasize how happy and proud we are to have our own unique hands. Always be aware of those children who may have physical disabilities.

Continue by having the children wiggle their fingers, wave their hands, and shake the hand of a friend. Share the ways our hands can express our love and joy for one another.

◆ **Acting Justly.** Direct the children to open their books to page 63. Recall that we all looked at our hands. Ask how the pictured hands are used for working, eating, loving, helping, and playing. Make sure that the children tell what is happening in each of the pictures.

• Teach the first verse of the Theme Song, "Helping Hands."

Let volunteers share ways their hands help them to play and, especially, to care. Allow time for the children to share their stories and examples. Point to the happy faces of the children in the book. It is fun to use our hands to play. It also feels good to work at something with our hands, to accomplish something special. And when we help family members or friends, we know we are doing good things with our hands.

◆ **Praying Together.** As the children walk to the prayer center and gather around the table, lead them in a little clapping march. As the children hold hands, conduct the following prayer:

Catechist: Dear God, thank you for our helping hands.

All: Thank you, God, for our hands.

Catechist: Our hands are for working and eating.

All: Thank you, God, for our hands.

Catechist: Our hands are for loving and playing.

All: Thank you, God, for our hands. Amen.

*Our hands express our love
and joy for one another.
How?*

*What are some ways that
you give others a helping
hand?*

Day 2

◆ **Gathering Together.** Begin by singing the first verse of the Theme Song, "Helping Hands." You may want to make a new list of things we can do with our hands—play piano, play guitar, ride a bike—at the beginning of each day this week. Not only will each be an enjoyable, initial activity, but each presentation will serve to highlight to the children the uses of their hands.

◆ **Sharing Together.** The text on page 64 presents a helping hand story for the children to enjoy. You are the storyteller. How well you animate the story with your facial expressions and role-playing will greatly affect its charm and impact.

First, invite the group to look at the illustration and guess what may be happening. Have them guess who the characters are. Then tell the story to the children. Emphasize the dramatic words. Be sure to enjoy the story yourself.

You may want to reinforce the theme of the story by having the children pretend to be Gramps, Grandma, Julia, and Tommy. Include some neighbors or friends in order to have as many children participate as possible. Encourage the "actors" to go beyond the written story by adding their own endings or details. They might make up an entirely new story that tells about helping hands.

• Sensitively point out that some people may not have hands due to accidents or birth defects. These people help others in different ways.

◆ **Acting Justly.** Page 65 reaffirms the uniqueness of the children and their hands. Have them draw a hand or trace an outline of one of their own hands in the space provided.

You might help the children place one hand on a sponge saturated with fingerpaint, place the hand on a sheet of paper, and then paste the imprint on page 65. If this is done, do a second imprint to use during the Day 4 session.

Allow time for the children and you to compare hand drawings, outlines, or imprints. Let them walk around and see what your hand and the hands of the other children look like. Mingle among the children and compliment them on their artistic work. Then invite them to suggest ways that they could give someone a helping hand. Emphasize the joy we feel when we are able to give someone a helping hand.

◆ **Praying Together.** Have everyone hold hands and form a circle. Conclude with a brief prayer. Sing the first verse of the Theme Song, "Helping Hands," as part of your prayer time.

As a closing hymn you may wish to teach "Jesus, Jesus" from the *Hymnal for Catholic Students*, #143.

Day 3

◆ **Gathering Together.** Begin by singing the first verse of the Theme Song, "Helping Hands." Review with the group some things we can do with our hands. We can work, eat, play, and help others. Let several children recollect how they can give someone a helping hand. Remind them of the story of Gramps. We can always use our hands to help someone.

◆ **Sharing Together.** Have the children open their books as you read aloud page 66. Ask the children to name all the things they see people doing with their hands. Ask for examples of how we use our hands to work, at play, at school, at home, and with our friends.

• Continue the discussion by asking for other examples of how we can help others with our hands. Have the children look at the illustration of the girl with the rake on page 67. Ask, "How is she helping her family?" Talk about how we can always help others wherever we are.

As the children comment on the pictures on pages 66 and 67, emphasize the fun there is found in knowing all that we can do with our hands.

◆ **Acting Justly.** Divide the children into pairs and distribute sheets of construction paper that you have folded in half to each pair of children. Help the first partner of each pair to trace the outline of his or her left hand with the thumb touching the fold. Turn the paper over to help the second partner trace his or her right hand with the thumb also touching the fold.

Now assist the children in cutting around the outlines of their hands so that when the paper is opened up, there are two hands joined at the thumbs. Encourage the pairs to draw themselves inside their hand outlines. The drawings should show how they can help their partner at work or play. After all the pairs have completed their drawings, let each come up to the front of the room to share what she or he has drawn. Allow plenty of time for the children to explain how they can help others.

◆ **Praying Together.** Lead the children to the prayer center and conduct a brief prayer of thanksgiving for all we can do with our hands. You may wish to include the Theme Song, "Helping Hands," as part of the prayer service.

Your hands are unique. There is not another pair of hands like them in the whole world.

Who are some people who have given you a helping hand?

How is the Sign of Peace expressed in your parish?

Hands are powerful ways to express love and care and thanks.

Day 4

◆ **Gathering Together.** Begin by singing the first verse of the Theme Song, "Helping Hands." As the children get settled, recall with them some of the things we can do with our hands when we work and when we play. Inquire if any of the children have used their hands in a helping way since the last time you met together. Have them tell how they used their hands. Maybe a friend needed a hand on the playground after school. If examples such as these did occur, congratulate the children on actually doing what they learned.

◆ **Sharing Together.** Have the children make a hand collage for your bulletin board that will highlight the session's theme of using our hands. Obtain objects of varying textures; for example, sandpaper, flannel, velvet, burlap, and plastic. Also gather tiny pebbles and paper clips that the children can paste or glue to form a border around a large sheet of sturdy construction paper. Have them paste or glue their handprint pictures within the border.

If the children made an extra handprint during the Day 2 session, have them cut around the imprints and paste them in collage fashion around the pictures. The children could add drawings of themselves and other children using their hands at work or play. Print the title, "Thank You, God, for Our Hands," on the collage.

◆ **Acting Justly.** Invite the children to share what they will do to lend someone a helping hand. Have the children give specific ideas from their own lives. These examples need not be overpowering. A simple little act of kindness will be much appreciated. Encourage the children to do what they have set out to do.

• As the children look at their lively collage, read aloud its title, "Thank You, God, for Our Hands." Pause for a few quiet moments. The children have just created a wonderful piece of art that expresses joy and thanksgiving. They did it together with the use of their hands. Those small hands of theirs were able to do something for all to see, to create something that touches others.

Let the children understand all this and reflect on it for a brief moment. Using our hands is a powerful way to express love and care and thanks. Urge the children to thank God in their hearts for the gift of their expressive hands.

◆ **Praying Together.** The prayer service on page 68 reinforces all the good that we can express with our hands. Have the children pray the Sign of the Cross. Follow the annotations in the Guide for directions about the lectionary.

• You may wish to teach the hymn "Jesus, Jesus" from the *Hymnal for Catholic Students,* #143.

PART TWO
JESUS' HELPING HANDS

God's Word

The "laying on of hands," is a power-laden gesture. What are some life situations in which the use of touch brings great healing?

What images do you find in the Gospels that show how Jesus' hands were filled with power?

Journeying in Faith

The Bible uses a number of idioms that refer to hands. In these figures of speech, hands frequently represent power and strength. Like other ancient peoples, the Israelites regarded the hand as the extension of the self, a manifestation of one's own person.

The scriptures speak of "the hand of Yahweh," and attribute to it the ability to write, to touch, to strike down, and to build up. But they are careful to distinguish God's power from that of humans. The hand of Yahweh refers not to the means or instrument through which God accomplished something, but to God's omnipotence. This involves the unlimited control of the entire universe and all it contains. Remember the words of the old song, "He's got the whole wide world in his hands, in his hands." Think about what they really mean.

The Bible also sees the human hand as a manifestation of strength and authority. The "laying on of hands," for example, is a power-laden gesture. It establishes a direct contact between two persons. Power passes from one to the other. The book of Genesis describes the touching scene when Jacob adopted two of his grandsons as his own. He stretched out his right hand and laid it on Ephraim's head. Crossing his hands, he laid his left hand on Manasseh's head.

Similarly, in the gospel accounts, we find that the laying on of hands is a way of showing both acceptance and the giving of self. As with Jacob, it accompanies prayer, as is evident in the story of Jesus and the children: "Some people brought children to Jesus for him to place his hands on them and to pray for them. . ." (Matthew 19:13–15).

Elsewhere, we read that healing power radiates from Jesus through touch. Remember the story of the leper. Jesus stretched out his hand, touched him, and the leper was made clean. And there was the woman who had suffered from hemorrhages for twelve years. She had heard what people were saying about Jesus. She said to herself that if I touch even his clothes, I shall be cured. Jesus said it was her faith that cured her. She felt power coming forth from him.

The importance of the "personal touch" for cementing human relationships is nowhere better illustrated than in the parable of the Good Samaritan. When he spotted the victim of a mugging lying along the highway, the Samaritan could have done several things. He could have passed by, like the priest and the Levite who did not want to get involved. He could have gone to find someone who knew the victim and to notify the police.

61

What would you have done in the case of the Good Samaritan?

The Good Samaritan went up and bandaged his wounds, bathing them with oil and wine. Then he lifted him onto his own beast, brought him to an inn, and looked after him there. The traditional hatred between the Jews and their Samaritan rivals to the north gives the story bite, but it should not be forgotten that Jesus told the parable to illustrate what neighborliness is. Neighborliness includes the involvement of self, getting one's hands dirty in helping others.

Commentaries on the gospel of Luke, where the story of the Good Samaritan appears, emphasize the point by linking it with the incident that follows. Jesus visited the house of a woman named Martha. She was free from the selfishness that seeks its own pleasure and convenience. Martha had a real concern for others. But for all her good works, she is gently chided by Jesus for forgetting to give personal attention to her guest.

What personal experiences have you had that speak to the power of touch?

The importance of the personal touch runs through the gospels, but no place is the message more explicit than when Jesus washes the feet of his disciples and dries them with a towel. After washing their feet and taking his garments again, he sat down. "Do you understand what I have just done to you?" he asked. "You call me Teacher and Lord, and it is right that you do so, because that is what I am. I, your Lord and Teacher, have just washed your feet. You, then, should wash one another's feet. I have set an example for you, so that you will do just what I have done for you" (John 13: 12–15).

Dear Catechist,

Most family celebrations are made up of familiar actions. But there is usually something surprising about them also. We sing "Happy Birthday," give gifts, carve and share the turkey, decorate the Christmas tree, kiss under the mistletoe. We expect these actions as part of our celebration on these occasions. But we also look forward to the surprise. What gift will we receive? Who will come? Something old and something new are part of all our rituals.

Prayer celebrations also contain familiar symbolic actions of the Christian community. We process, sing, stand, sit, listen, speak, hug, shake hands, share food and drink. These actions involve us, body and spirit, in our prayer. By repeating symbolic actions in our prayer, we come to know and love their meaning. The handshake or kiss of peace was at one time an awkward experience for many of us. Today many of us would feel slighted if we did not have it.

The more children engage in ritual action, like standing for the gospel reading or blessing themselves, the more they will become at ease with community prayer. If they learn how to participate in ritual prayer through their catechesis, they will be ready to participate with the Sunday assembly. If their experience of prayer in catechesis is a positive one, the children will joyfully anticipate other prayer experiences. And they will be ready for them. With such experiences will grow the desire and the need for community prayer.

Sr. Anne Marie

JESUS' HELPING HANDS

God's Word

Journeying in Faith with Children

Aims

- To discover ways we talk with our hands
- To share the story of the Good Samaritan
- To share the story of Jesus washing the feet of his friends
- To review the Our Father

New Words

good neighbor

Materials

Day 1: • musical instrument
- toy instrument
- Bible

Day 2: • none

Day 3: • Bible

Day 4: • crayons or pencils
- flannel figures (optional)

Theme Song

"Helping Hands" from the cassette *Songs for Living Waters 1* by Stephen Chapin

Day 1

◆ **Gathering Together.** If possible, bring in a stringed instrument, such as a guitar or violin, or perhaps a horn with valves, such as a trumpet. You might receive help from an adult or older child in demonstrating how the instruments are played. Talk about the ways musicians use their hands to play music. The children can use their hands to produce "music" on a toy instrument.

◆ **Sharing Together.** Now invite the children to open their books to page 69. As they enjoy looking at the musician, baker, and carpenter, have volunteers tell how the hands of these people help us. Perhaps some in the group have actually seen hands do these activities. If so, let them share how they were helped by the experiences. This could lead to ways the children help with their own hands. As always, all examples, however simple, should be complimented.

◆ **Acting Justly.** Hold up the Bible for all to see. Ask what this special book is called. Say something, such as: "That's right! We call our special book the Bible. It has many wonderful stories about Jesus. There are many stories in our Bible about how Jesus helped people and about how people used their hands to help someone in need."

• Ask the children to tell about times when they have seen someone give help to another person. Highlight instances of people giving food and clothing to the homeless or victims of a natural disaster.

◆ **Praying Together.** If a musician is present, you may invite him or her to play some lovely background music as the children gather in the prayer center. You may then direct the musician to accompany the group as you all sing a favorite song. Then conduct the following prayer:

Catechist: Dear Jesus, thank you for hands that help us.

All Sing: Alleluia! Alleluia!

Catechist: Dear Jesus, thank you for our hands that help others.

All Sing: Alleluia! Alleluia!

Catechist: Dear Jesus, thank you for showing us how to use our helping hands.

All Sing: Alleluia! Alleluia!

Jesus showed us how to use our hands to help each other. What is the best thing you do with your hands?

We can always ask God to give us the strength to help others.

Day 2

◆ **Gathering Together.** Recall how hands can help us and how we can help others with our hands. Perhaps some of the children have offered a helping hand or have been given a helping hand since you last met. By all means, let them share their experiences. Point out that there are always opportunities for us to help others. And when we do so, we show not only our love for the person we helped but also our love for Jesus.

◆ **Sharing Together.** Have the children turn to pages 70 and 71 and allow time for them to enjoy the drama of the illustration. Perhaps some will guess what is happening in the picture. As in previous sessions, animate the story as you tell it. This story has a realistic power to it. The traveler in the Bible is not some prettified, remote character but someone you could see or hear about today. As in our society, there were those who saw and did not want to get involved.

As you read about the man from Samaria, emphasize the dramatic words in the story. His heart was filled with sadness. He gently washed the man's wounds and bandaged them. He put the man on his own animal. Not only did this good man do all this, but he also offered to pay for the victim to get well.

Do not rush your narration. This is a story you have heard many times, but it might be the first time the children have heard it. Emphasize how physically hard the work of helping was for the good man. Point out that by the work of his hands, he showed the bigness of his heart. By giving a helping hand, we show we love Jesus, ourselves, and one another.

◆ **Acting Justly.** The questions on page 71 continue to lead the children to an appreciation of a caring, helping community. Emphasize that Jesus always gave people a helping hand. We can always ask Jesus to give us the love and the strength to help others.

• Teach the second verse of the Theme Song, "Helping Hands."

◆ **Praying Together.** Lead the following prayer service:

Catechist: Thank you, Jesus, for all your stories about helping hands.

All: We are good neighbors! (Extend hands outward.)

Catechist: When we see someone who needs our help, let us give a helping hand.

All: We are good neighbors! (Extend hands overhead.)

Catechist: Dear Jesus, you always gave people a helping hand. Help us to help others.

All: We are good neighbors! (Extend hands downward.)

Day 3

◆ **Gathering Together.** Begin by holding the Bible up for all to see. Recall how we already have heard some wonderful stories that are in our Bible. Review the main points of yesterday's story of the Good Samaritan. Sing the first two verses of the Theme Song, "Helping Hands."

◆ **Sharing Together.** As the group looks at the illustration on page 72, mention that by his actions Jesus showed how much he loved people. It is always easier to say you love someone or to promise to help out a friend. By actually giving someone a helping hand, we show by our actions our love for that person.

As you begin telling the story on page 72, point to Jesus washing his friend's feet. Emphasize the descriptive details in the story for the children: Everyone had walked a long time on the hot, dusty roads. They were all tired and dirty. Jesus knew how his friends felt. He cared about them so much that he wanted to do something to show his love. Point out that Jesus wanted to show his friends how they should treat one another. So he washed their feet. Relate the story to parents or family who take care of us when we are tired.

◆ **Acting Justly.** Continue discussing page 72 by highlighting the words, "I have given you an example, so that you will do for others just what I have done for you." Ask the children what they think Jesus meant when he said these words to his friends. Ask the children to recall kind things others have done for them. Ask how they could do the same for a loved one who gave them a helping hand. Ask for responses to the questions on page 72.

◆ **Praying Together.** Remind the children that their hands can do many things. Then pray together. (Sensitively adapt the prayer if there are children who do not have the use of their hands.)

Catechist: Let us thank Jesus for our helping hands.

All: Thank you, Jesus.

Catechist: Thank you, Jesus, for our hands that hold our books and feed our pets.

All: Thank you, Jesus.

Catechist: Thank you, Jesus, for our hands that print and color and touch and hug.

All: Thank you, Jesus.

Catechist: But most of all, thank you, Jesus, for our hands that help others.

All: Thank you, Jesus, for our helping hands.

Conclude by singing the first two verses of the Theme Song, "Helping Hands."

By his actions Jesus showed how much he loved people. "I have set an example for you." How do you respond?

Day 4

What will you do today to be a helping hand to someone?

◆ **Gathering Together.** Begin by singing the first two verses of the Theme Song, "Helping Hands." Have the children turn to page 73 in their books. This page invites the children to get specific about what they have heard this week in our two biblical stories. Take the time to review the two stories that they have heard. The use of flannelboard characters would help you with the review. Or let the children role-play the two stories. Keep everyone focused on the theme of hands that help others.

◆ **Sharing Together.** After reviewing the biblical stories, invite the children to tell what is happening in each of the pictures on page 73. If time permits, let other children who did not role-play earlier act out the situations pictured and have the rest of the group share how the children are doing what Jesus wants us to do.

◆ **Acting Justly.** Now direct the group's attention to the blank space on page 73. Ask the question, "How will you be a helping hand to someone?" Urge them to think of one way that they could show a helping hand to someone today or tonight at home. In other words, encourage them to think and draw in a very specific way.

Who has been a helping hand to you recently?

If necessary, lead the children through the next few hours of the day to highlight ways that they might show a helping hand. Perhaps Janie could help her mom bring in baby brother's stroller this afternoon, or Andy could help wash the dishes.

After everyone has finished drawing, allow sufficient time for each child to share his or her drawing. Point out that what we learn about during our time together can make a real difference in all of our lives. Perhaps Janie will notice her mother's look of surprise and delight. Andy might just feel good that he's helped out, that he has accomplished something.

◆ **Praying Together.** Have the children hold hands as you lead them through the prayer celebration on page 74. At each phrase of blessing, invite the children to raise their joined hands in praise to God. Follow the directions given in the annotations.

As a closing hymn, you may wish to teach "Jesus, Jesus" from the *Hymnal for Catholic Students,* #143.

HANDS THAT HELP OTHERS

The Church

Men and women are called to be collaborators or co-creators with God in the on-going work of creation. In what ways is this so?

The helping hand of another, whether friend or stranger, is also a healing hand. How have you been healed by the touch of a stranger?

Journeying in Faith

We have all seen diagrams picturing the evolution of the human hand. The high school science books told us that our hands and fingers, especially the thumb, have been important in the evolution of the human race. Because of the way our hands developed, we can accomplish things other living creatures cannot do.

According to an ancient Indian legend, it is our hands that make us most like God. Some Christian theologians say that when God made human beings in God's "own image and likeness," God meant for them to also be "makers." Men and women are called to be collaborators or co-creators with God in the on-going work of creation. How does this make you feel?

Modern technology, which has done much to improve the world around us, is a combination of brain power and manual skills. We seldom think how much we are indebted to Louis Pasteur, Thomas Edison, Henry Ford and others whose inventions have revolutionized the way we live. Only God knows the part they have played in the building up of the Kingdom of God on earth.

Machines are the extension of human hands. The primitive stone knives of prehistoric times, like the intricate mechanical and electronic devices of today, have been designed to increase and improve what we can manufacture. *Manufacture* is another term for "hand made"!

Farm machinery, such as plows, reapers, and combines, help us to raise more food, so we can feed not only the people in our own country, but so we can export grain to less fortunate nations. Knitting mills have made it possible for millions of people to have fine clothes. Assembly lines manufacture a variety of consumer products, from detergents to television sets. These have all come to be taken for granted.

There are some things, however, machines cannot do. Machines cannot express love and concern. No machine, for example, is capable of providing a "personal touch." Only human hands can caress us, smooth away the wrinkles of worry in our face, or hold our hand to reassure us. The helping hand of another, whether friend or stranger, is also a healing hand.

In what creative ways do you use your hands to heal and help?

Christians, at least the saints, have always been characterized by their personal touch. "See how they love one another." Coming in all sizes and ages, from every segment of society and walk of life, the saints have this common characteristic—their willingness to serve others. Even kings and queens engaged in the kind of activities that we associate today with social work and practical nursing. St. Elizabeth of Hungary anticipated "meals-on-wheels" by taking food to shut-ins. St. Camillus de Lellis, a sometime soldier of fortune and gambler, ministered to the bodily care of the sick and infirm. Repelled by the unsightliness of a leper, Francis found his whole life turned around when he ministered to the unfortunate man with his own hands.

The saints used their hands in creative ways. When St. Louise de Marillac recognized the needs of the poor and the sick, she gathered other women to help her minister to those who were in need. Louise's followers were eventually named the Daughters of Charity. These women, in the name of Christ, cared for orphans, the aged, and the mentally handicapped. They began and staffed hospitals as nurses. They performed these works of charity long before the state or the government became involved in this kind of care.

Our hands and hearts are needed to carry on God's work. Do you believe this? If so, what difference does it make in your life?

As is evident in all of God's dealings with the world, especially in the Incarnation, God chooses to heal and save us in a human way. God calls upon Christians to continue the work of building up the kingdom on earth. God depends on us to be collaborators and co-creators. Our hands and hearts are needed to carry on God's work.

Hands That Help Others

Journeying in Faith with Children

The Church

Aims

- To recall the many ways hands can be used to help
- To discover how Saint Francis helped others
- To discover how Saint Louise de Marillac helped others
- To decide how to give a helping hand to others

New Word

healing

Materials

Day 1: • none
Day 2: • none
Day 3: • none
Day 4: • large, sturdy paper
  • crayons or markers
  • notepaper
  • candle

Theme Song

"Helping Hands" from the cassette *Songs for Living Waters 1* by Stephen Chapin

Day 1

◆ **Gathering Together.**   Begin by singing the first two verses of the Theme Song, "Helping Hands." Review the story of Jesus washing the feet of his friends. Direct the group's attention to page 75. Let the children use their imaginations to tell what has happened in the scene and how they think the child feels.

◆ **Sharing Together.**   Read the first two lines. Ask the children to circle the helping hands and tell why these hands are helping hands. Emphasize that Christians bring God's love and care with their helping hands. As the children respond to the question "Has anything like this ever happened to you?" listen closely. You will learn much about each child's experience with caregivers.

Some of the children will readily relate to the situation. Some may already have been hurt themselves or been sick and in need of help. Emphasize the question "Who helps you feel better when you are sick?" Remember that it is not the sickness that is in focus, but the people who are there to help with their hands and their love.

◆ **Acting Justly.**   Continue discussing first-grade experiences that may require a helping hand, such as: A child rushes around the house and bangs into a wall, and a parent or guardian is there to soothe the hurt.

• Try to elicit from the children situations in which they offered a friend a comforting hug or gentle words of love and concern. Reinforce the concept that helping others is a process of giving and receiving.

◆ **Praying Together.**   Close with the following prayer:

Catechist: Dear Jesus, thank you for our hands that help others.

All: Thanks be to God.

Catechist: Dear Jesus, thank you for all our loved ones who help us feel better when we are sick.

All: Thanks be to God.

Catechist: Dear Jesus, let us, as Christians, bring God's love and care to those who need a helping hand.

All: Thanks be to God. Amen.

It is the mind and heart and person behind the hands that expresses God's love in the world.

Were you ever sick as a child? Whose hands nursed you back to health? What do you remember about those hands?

Day 2

◆ **Gathering Together.** Recall that yesterday we talked about times when we were hurt or sick and someone helped us to feel better. Remind the children of some of the examples they gave yesterday. Explain that Christians always try to bring God's love and care by giving those in need a helping hand. Christians do this every day.

◆ **Sharing Together.** Point out that today we are going to hear a story about a special Christian who lived a long time ago. His name was Francis, and he brought God's love to many people with his helping hands. After the children turn to pages 76 and 77, call their attention to the colorful border around the pages, and let them discover the birds and buildings of Francis' time. Be sure they enjoy Francis' horse with its rich trappings and the luxury of Francis' clothes and appearance. These highlight the great wealth of Francis and his family.

Read pages 76 and 77 to the children. Invite them to respond to the question on page 77. Some of your children may not like the countenance of the sick man. He is not meant to look pretty. The contrast between the two figures will tell the story as vividly as your talent in being the experienced storyteller that you are by now.

• Teach the third verse of the Theme Song, "Helping Hands."

◆ **Acting Justly.** After telling the story, lead the children in a discussion that brings the sick man to a street in their own neighborhood. Ask, "How many would bother to help or even look in his direction?" Depending on where the children live, they may or may not have seen the homeless and the sick. The point of the story is that the situation told of Francis holds true for people today just as it did for people who lived long ago. If the children understand the timeliness of Francis' care and concern, much has been accomplished.

• The sick, unsightly man asked, "Help me in the name of Jesus." And despite his aversion, Francis did help the man. "He washed the man and bandaged his sores," which was an extraordinary, deeply human thing to do. From that day forward, Francis became a living example of how God's love can be brought to everyone. His hands did the acts of kindness that changed his heart forever.

◆ **Praying Together.** Conclude with the following prayer:

Catechist: Dear God, thank you for our friend, Saint Francis. Francis' helping hands brought your love to everyone he met. Whenever we meet someone who needs God's love, let us have hands like Saint Francis.

All: Amen.

Day 3

◆ **Gathering Together.** As the children get settled, offer a brief opening prayer to celebrate Saint Francis. The prayer might thank God for giving us Francis who used his hands to show God's love for everyone. Sing all the verses of the Theme Song, "Helping Hands."

Review the main points of Francis' story. Explain that we have many stories of Christians who have used their hands to make people feel better. Today, we will hear another one of these stories.

◆ **Sharing Together.** Have the children open their books to the story of Saint Louise de Marillac on page 78. Louise was a young woman who had been sick as a child. There may be children in your group who have a background similar to Louise de Marillac's. If they offer to share their stories, ask who gave them a helping hand when they were sick.

Read the story of Saint Louise de Marillac on page 78.

• The story of Louise is not only another example of someone who cared for others, but also the story about the growth of a community of people who cared for the sick and the homeless. From this one woman's concern came the Daughters of Charity and all the hospitals and homes for the needy that still help others today. Bring the group to the realization that each child's simple act of caring can influence other children and adults to also care. Helping hands linked together are a powerful force.

◆ **Acting Justly.** The two questions at the bottom of page 78 are designed to relate the story of Louise to the children's own acts of helping hands. As the children talk about times they helped take care of someone who was sick, write these on the chalkboard. An example might be bringing soup to someone who is sick or being quiet at play so as not to disturb the sick person. Have the children suggest other ways.

◆ **Praying Together.** Conclude by saying a brief prayer in which you thank God for our ability to help others with our hands. Again, sing all the verses of the Theme Song, "Helping Hands." Invite the children to add actions to interpret the words.

How does Francis' situation hold true today?

The hands of St. Louise did the acts of kindness that changed many people's lives.

A sad face can turn into a happy face because of our love and concern. What examples have you had of this experience?

Help us, Lord, to learn how to lend a hand to those who need our help.

Day 4

◆ **Gathering Together.** Offer a short prayer of thanks for learning stories about two such loving and caring people as Francis and Louise. Whenever we see someone in need, we can remember their stories and treat everyone the way they did.

Review the stories of Francis and Louise. Be certain to ask how Saint Francis used his hands to bring God's love to others and how Saint Louise and the Daughters of Charity brought healing love to sick people and to children who had no families.

◆ **Sharing Together.** Have the children open their books to page 79. This page encourages the children to reflect on those people who have helped them. As they draw and talk about the people who helped them, the concept of helping hands as a two-way process of giving and receiving will be strengthened and made real.

Allow plenty of time for each child to tell the story of his or her drawing. Ask questions, such as: Where are you? Who is there to help you? What happened to you? Were you sick or did you fall and hurt yourself? How did you feel when someone cared enough about you to offer a helping hand to make you feel better? Emphasize the last question. Explain that what we do affects others and that how others treat us, especially when we are in need, affects us.

◆ **Acting Justly.** Suggest to the children one way to act justly in your neighborhood, here and now. Surely there are members of your parish who are sick or bedridden or in need of some love and attention. Perhaps there is a nursing home that will cooperate with you, or you might know of some elderly people who would welcome a hello from some first graders.

Have the children create a greeting card. Obtain a large piece of tagboard or sturdy construction paper that is big enough for all the children to draw on. They may want to make a colorful, wide border like the one on pages 76 and 77. They could draw their faces, where they live, birds or trees, or just lively designs. Compose a group note to paste in the center to tell the recipients that the children used their hands to make this cheerful card special. Help the children to print their names around the message.

◆ **Praying Together.** Have the children gather in a circle around the table in the prayer center. Light the candle. Then go through each phrase of the service on page 80. Have a brief moment of quiet as you begin the prayer celebration. Follow the directions in the annotations.

You may wish to close with the hymn "Jesus, Jesus" from the *Hymnal for Catholic Students,* #143.

WE PRAY WITH OUR HANDS

We Pray

How do you express yourself with your hands? How do you use your hands in prayer?

Our open hands say that we are receptive to whatever God will send.

Journeying in Faith

One of the earliest forms in Christian art is a figure with outstretched arms and palms turned upward. The figure is called an *orans,* "a petitioner." It appears in the ancient catacombs, and before that, it is found in the art of various pagan temples.

Praying with outstretched hands is a natural, spontaneous gesture. Empty hands express need. Open hands symbolize an open heart. Patient hands suggest that if we are willing to wait long enough, the Lord will come.

Perseverance in prayer is also shown by the hands. The Bible tells the story of the battle between the Israelites and the people of Amalek. While Joshua led the Israelite warriors into battle, Moses prayed with outstretched arms. Whenever Moses raised his hands, Israel had the advantage, and when he lowered his hands, Amalek had the advantage. As the story goes, Moses grew weary, but Aaron and Hur propped up his arms until sunset when Joshua, with Yahweh's help, was able to win the battle.

At Mass, the priest takes the posture of the orans. He petitions God in the name of the community. He prays the Lord's Prayer, standing with outstretched arms and hands opened upward. In the early Church and in some places even today, the whole congregation does the same when saying the Lord's Prayer. Our upright posture speaks reverence. Our empty hands indicate need. "Give us this day our daily bread." Our open hands say that we are receptive to whatever God will send.

But there are other gestures which our hands also use to speak the language of prayer.

Folded hands, fingers pointed heavenward, speak reverent adoration. They seem like Gothic spires to lift our whole being upward, out of ourselves.

Hands and arms crossed over our heart is more an inward gesture. It suggests a dedication of self, an attentive quiet before the movement of God's grace within.

Another very human gesture that Christians adopted centuries ago is striking one's breast. It is like pinching ourselves to make us wake up to our faults and responsibilities. Mea culpa. I have sinned through my own fault in thought, word, and deed. Lord, have mercy on me.

In recent years, in North America at least, it has become customary to offer a sign of peace by extending the hand of friendship to those near us. We embrace one another as a sign of our acceptance of each other.

When do you pray the Sign of the Cross? Is it a favorite prayer for you?

The Sign of the Cross is an ancient prayer. For centuries, children have been learning it almost as soon as they are able to talk. "In the Name of the Father, Son, and Holy Spirit." Words joined with gesture. The movement of the hand from forehead to breast, from the left to right shoulder, speaks a kind of "body language" of its own.

The Sign of the Cross is used at the beginning of prayer—the Mass, the rosary—because it is a way of pulling us all together, of gathering up our thoughts and feelings as we turn our minds and hearts to God. It is the sign of our redemption, embracing as it were our whole person from the tips of our fingers to the very innermost heart of our being. It is a reminder that by his death on the cross, Jesus liberated us—body and spirit—from the power of sin.

Many Christians make the Sign of the Cross in time of danger, that it may protect and strengthen them. At Mass and in the sacrament of penance, bishops and priests bless us with the Sign of the Cross, saying that we receive the fullness of life from God. The Sign of the Cross has so many possible explanations that it is no wonder it became a Christian symbol almost from the beginning.

Pray the Lord's Prayer with gestures. Feel the beauty and power we experience when we pray with our whole being.

Receiving communion in the hand is an ancient practice which has recently been restored. Lifting up and extending the hand to receive the Lord is a prayer that acknowledges need and receptivity. Feeding oneself is a response to Christ's instruction—take and eat.

During the next few moments, say the Lord's Prayer slowly, and use the appropriate hand gestures. Think about each line as it is expressed by your hand movements. Feel the beauty and power we experience when we pray with our whole being.

We Pray with Our Hands

We Pray

Journeying in Faith with Children

Aims

- To discover ways we talk with our hands
- To discover ways we can pray with our hands
- To determine ways we pray with our hands at Mass
- To review the Our Father with gestures

New Words

signing
praying
Sign of Peace

Materials

Day 1: • book on signing
- braille book
- objects of various shapes and textures
- shoebox

Day 2: • none

Day 3: • paper plates
- glue or paste
- "Our Father" sheets
- yarn
- crayons or markers

Day 4: • none

Theme Song

"Helping Hands" from the cassette *Songs for Living Waters 1* by Stephen Chapin

Day 1

◆ **Gathering Together.** Using only your hands, direct the children to stand up and fold their hands in prayer. Then say aloud, "Dear God, help us to talk not only with our words but also with our hands. Amen."

◆ **Sharing Together.** Direct the children to open their books to page 81. Have them look at the picture of the children signing, or talking with their hands. Let volunteers share what they think the children are saying with their hands. Ask what each of the hand signs means. Explain that we can talk to others without words through our hands.

• This will lead to a presentation on "signing." You may have children in your group who cannot hear or the children may have friends who cannot hear. Emphasize the wonderful ways children who are deaf can talk with their hands. Teach the children to sign "Hello" or "I love you."

> *OPTIONAL.* If possible, allow the children to feel and "read" a book written in braille. As we have celebrated the gifts of our wonderful hands, we need to be aware of those of us who may not have full use of hands, ears, or eyes.

◆ **Acting Justly.** Obtain objects of various textures and shapes. Place the objects inside a shoebox, on one side of which you have cut a hole large enough for a child to put his or her hand through. Show a simple drawing of an object and ask a child to place a hand inside the box, feel for the item, and describe it. This will continue to help the child appreciate how the sense of touch can help a blind person to "see" the world. If the children know people who are blind or deaf, ask them how these people should be treated.

◆ **Praying Together.** Pray this gestured prayer:

Catechist: Every time we make the Sign of the Cross, we pray with our hands. Let us pray our signing prayer together.

All: (Pray the Sign of the Cross.)

Catechist: Let us use our hands as we pray the Our Father together.

All: (Pray the Our Father with gestures.)

We talk not only with our words, but with our hands. How do you use your hands to talk to others?

Day 2

◆ **Gathering Together.** Recall that there are many ways that we can "talk" with our hands. Mention that when someone writes a book that is written in braille, the author talks to the reader who is blind by the use of the reader's fingers. Those who are blind read through their fingers.

◆ **Sharing Together.** Have the children turn to pages 82 and 83 in their books. Mention that we can talk to God with hand gestures just as we sometimes speak to one another with our hands. Let the children share what they think the children pictured on the pages are saying to God with their hands. Then have them match the drawing with the words by printing the number next to each phrase in its appropriate box.

Circulate among the children as they do this activity and gently help them make the correct matchups. The atmosphere here should be one of joy and discovery. Some already know the words and actions to the Sign of the Cross. They have all said and gestured the "Amen" in previous prayer services. The words *"Peace be with you"* and *"Alleluia"* have been heard at Mass. Some children will know them. Others will not.

How does your parish exchange the greeting of peace?

◆ **Acting Justly.** Introduce the Sign of Peace to the children. Show them how we do this prayer and invite them to say the words with you. Discuss what we mean when we say "Peace be with you." Consider different ways we can bring peace into our homes.

After the Sign of Peace has been presented, have the group practice giving a handshake of peace as they say the words *"Peace be with you."* Then have them say "Amen" with hands folded in prayer. At the conclusion of the service, the children can spread their hands and arms up high and say loudly "Alleluia!"

◆ **Praying Together.** Say the Sign of the Cross together. Ask the children to share the Sign of Peace with one another. Close with the Sign of the Cross. Sing all the verses of the Theme Song, "Helping Hands."

Day 3

◆ **Gathering Together.**   Begin by singing all the verses of the Theme Song, "Helping Hands." Review with the children each of the hand gestures on pages 82 and 83.

◆ **Sharing Together.**   Have the children turn to pages 84 and 85. These pages bring the children into the community of prayer at Mass. Go through each photograph one at a time. Ask what the two children in the picture at the bottom of page 84 might be praying. For example: are they saying "Hello" to God? Are they thanking God for their families?

The picture on the right of page 84 shows a child receiving the Eucharist by hand. Your group does not yet receive Holy Communion, but they most likely have seen others receiving it this way. Show them how they will hold out their hands when they do receive Holy Communion.

Using the picture on page 85, point out the hands of the priest leading the members of the parish assembly in the Our Father. Have the children note the people joining hands to pray the Lord's Prayer. We are all joined together at Mass with one another and with God. Emphasize the expressive hands that show reverence and love for God.

Ask if any of the children know a special prayer that Jesus taught his friends. It is, of course, the Our Father. Take sufficient time to go through every line of the prayer as often as your group needs to do so. Include the appropriate hand movements. Ask them to share the prayer and gestures with loved ones at home.

• Give each child a large paper plate with a hole punched in the top. Before this session, print the words to the Our Father on a sheet of paper and then make enough copies of the prayer for each child in the group. Cut out these sheets so that they fit within the paper plates. Paste a copy of the prayer on each of the plates.

◆ **Acting Justly.**   On the reverse side of the plate, invite the children to draw themselves individually praying with their hands. They might want to decorate around the prayer itself. Then run brightly colored yarn through each hole and tie it. The children can take their prayer plates home to share with their families. Encourage them to pray the Our Father at home with family members. Have them name ways they can reach out to others with their hands this week.

◆ **Praying Together.**   Gather everyone in the prayer center. Begin your prayer with the Sign of the Cross. Then ask for a moment of silence. Invite the children to think of their friends and loved ones at home who are always there to give them a helping hand. Pray to God to bless these wonderful people in our lives who do so much to help and care for each one of us.

God is always with us to listen to us. When do you talk to God? When do you listen to God?

We show reverence at Mass through the prayer of our hands.

How do you use your hands to offer praise to God?

Day 4

◆ **Gathering Together.** Discuss how we learned that people who cannot hear well or who cannot hear at all use signs to talk to us. Hands offer wonderful ways to express how and what we feel inside. Let the children practice some of the signs that they have learned. Ask if any in the group shared these signs with family.

◆ **Sharing Together.** Have different children explain the different gestures. Review with the group when we see these gestures and hear these words at Mass. Point out that we often say these phrases in our prayer celebrations. And we can pray, using these gestures, at any time and anywhere.

• Continue to invite the children to share how they have seen people use their hands to pray at Mass. Ask them what other gestures have they seen their priests use during Mass. Point out that all these gestures are signs of what we feel inside. Just as we hug a friend to show how much we love the friend, so we fold our hands or spread them way out in welcome or bless ourselves to show our love for God and one another.

◆ **Acting Justly.** Review the words of the Our Father and the gestures that accompany the words. Ask when the children will pray the Our Father: What times of day would they choose? The morning? Bedtime? Who will they ask to pray with them? Show how wonderful it is to pray with our family at home and with our parish family at Mass. We can always talk to God all by ourselves. God is always there to listen and talk to us.

• Review the major themes and make connections between all four parts of this chapter.

• Use pages 87 and 88 to highlight the major themes of this chapter.

• Sing all the verses of the Theme Song, "Helping Hands."

◆ **Praying Together.** The prayer service on page 86 offers another opportunity for the children to use their hands in prayer. Follow the annotations for the prayer service. To conclude, pray the Our Father with hand gestures.

You may wish to sing the hymn "Jesus, Jesus" from the *Hymnal for Catholic Students,* #143.

4.
Ears Are for Hearing

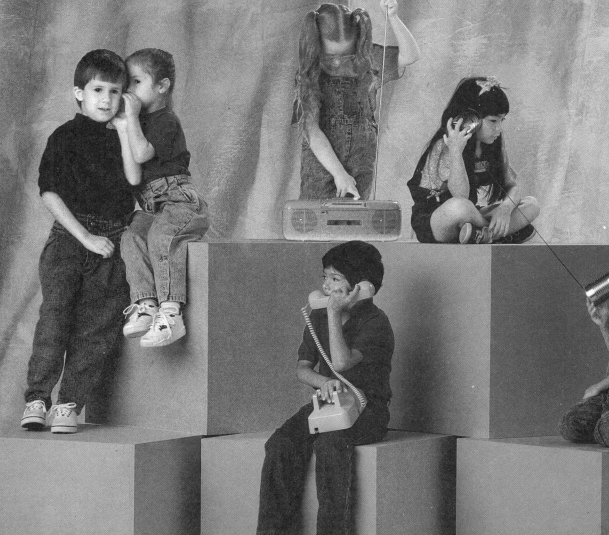

Looking Ahead

Listen carefully! What do you hear? In this chapter we will learn what our ears can do. Have you ever heard stories about Jesus? We will find out what Jesus is telling us in these stories.

Chapter Aims

OUR LIVES

To discover and appreciate the wonder of our ears for listening

GOD'S WORD

To learn about and appreciate the stories we listen to from the Bible and what we hear from them about God and about Jesus Christ

THE CHURCH

To appreciate that we listen to Jesus' teachings when the Gospels are read; we hear that we are to love God and others.

WE PRAY

To learn to be a good listener, especially at Mass; to learn the responses to the readings we hear at Mass

---

Chapter Four Theme Song

"We Can Hear" from the cassette *Songs for Living Waters 1* by Stephen Chapin

---

Using the Chapter Title Page

Invite the children to look with you at the picture on page 89, the Title Page of Chapter Four. Have them suggest what sounds each of the children in the picture might be hearing. Help them to appreciate that we can use these things because of the ability we have to hear.

Read the chapter title to the children and then preview the chapter by reading the "Looking Ahead" box. Take time for responses to the question.

Chapter Plan Ahead

Make arrangements for the following item well in advance of the session in which it is used.

• The optional activity calls for the lectionary used at Mass. (Part 4)

Music for the Prayer Services

"Listen to Us, O God," an original melody.

PART ONE
LISTENING

Our Lives

Listening requires effort and concentration. Would you rate yourself as a good listener?

Why is listening essential to growth?

Journeying in Faith

Listening is a cultivated art. There are some people who can listen to a motor and tell if it is working properly. Others listen to music with such a sensitive ear that they can immediately notice a faulty pitch. The sound of an orchestra tuning up is not music, but the trained ear of the musician brings forth clear and vibrant tones from the chaos that tuning up seems to be.

Our world is filled with sound: the song of the birds, the howl of the wind, the patter of the rain on the window. The constant refrains of motors and human voices reverberate in our ears. Because they are such a continuing refrain, we often do not hear them. The hum of the fan or air-conditioner is cut off by a deliberate decision not to hear.

"Not-hearing" is a protective device which we intentionally use. Not-hearing the surrounding sounds enables us to concentrate and to live without the intrusion that these sounds make on us. Not-hearing enables us to have some peace.

The problem is that the common practice of shutting off sound becomes a habit that interferes with our listening. We do not listen to voices or what the voices are saying to us. Members of our family or friends are cut off from communication with us because we are not listening. Listening requires effort and concentration.

In the days before the invention of the printing press, most people learned whatever they knew by listening. They listened to public speakers, to orators, and to storytellers. They heard troubadours sing stories of bravery and romance, of happiness and sorrow. They listened to teachers. From listening, they gained a knowledge of what the world and their own private world was like.

Careful, discriminative listening was essential for learning. What was heard had to be remembered. Remembering what was heard was of consequence. History was transmitted by telling, by listening, by repeating what was heard. People listened attentively.

The spoken word enabled them to know about the past, to describe the present, to project what the future might be. It empowered them to understand reality. The power to listen, and listen well, was essential for growth.

Listening takes us out of our own world and into the world of another. What sounds transport you most pleasantly?

How will you cultivate the art of listening?

Today we live in a world in which we are inundated with sounds, not only the sounds of nature and technology, but also the sounds that this technology brings. We hear human voices wherever we go. The radio utters news twenty-four hours a day. The television is a refrain of human voices, some speaking words that free us, and others hawking brand goods as if they were the panacea for all ills.

We hear the human voice so often that silence, the absence of sound, is a surprising experience. Sometimes it frightens or oppresses us. Sounds, multiple and constant, are our natural habitat. As a result, we often forget how to listen.

Each one of us has experienced talking to another person who is not listening to us. Conversation requires not only one who speaks, but also one who listens. Without a listener, conversation cannot take place. What the listener hears is not only the words that the speaker utters, but also the tone of speaking, the inflection of the voice, the implied meaning. A listener is attentive to the speaker. The listener is not waiting, somewhat impatiently, for a chance to speak. The listener concentrates on the speaker and the person's words.

We would all like to be heard by this kind of a listener. But are we this kind of listener? Listening is a human art that requires effort. It demands a certain selflessness. Listening takes us out of our own world and into the world of another.

The husband who listens to his wife communicates love in an intensive way. The mother who really hears her daughter expresses care and concern for her. Listening to another, whether the other is joyful or sorrowful, is an indication of reverence for the other. Not-listening expresses distraction and lack of concern.

If you would be a listener and not just a hearer in today's world, you must practice listening. Think for a moment about the varied sounds you heard today. Did you hear the sounds that surrounded you? What voices did you hear? What were they saying to you? What sounds of nature did you hear? How long has it been since you listened to the sound of the birds?

Ears are for hearing. We have ears but do not hear. If we want to hear, we shall have to decide to listen. Listening is a human art that has to be cultivated.

PART ONE
LISTENING

Journeying in Faith with Children

Our Lives

Aims

- To develop an awareness of the sounds around us and an appreciation for the gift of hearing
- To develop an awareness of how to listen to people

New Word

sound

Materials

Day 1: • objects with which to make sounds
Day 2: • music box
  • picture of a farm
  • drawing paper
  • pencils or crayons
Day 3: • pencils or crayons
  • picture of children conversing
Day 4: • small musical instruments
  • tape of beautiful orchestral music (optional)
  • cutouts of an outline of a child's head
  • pencils or crayons

Theme Song

"We Can Hear" from the cassette *Songs for Living Waters 1* by Stephen Chapin

Day 1

◆ **Gathering Together.** Tell the children that today we are going to learn more about a gift that we all share and that we are using right now as you speak. Ask them to guess the gift you are speaking about. As a hint, place your hand behind your ear in a gesture of listening.

◆ **Sharing Together.** Ask the children to listen as you clap your hands to a certain rhythm. Clap the rhythm and invite the children to repeat it after you. Do several exercises to sharpen their sense of hearing. Discuss the importance of their listening if they are to be able to repeat the sounds.

Invite the children to play a hearing game. Ask them to close their eyes and listen carefully. Then make different sounds, such as crumpling paper, closing a door, writing on the chalkboard, and so on. After each sound, ask them to identify the sound and tell how it was made.

• Have the children open their books to page 91. Have them examine the pictures and tell about all the things they see that can make sounds. Call on several children to respond to the questions.

Talk with the children about the difference between sounds they might hear in the city and those they might hear in the country. Ask which of the pictures show sounds they might hear in the city and which show sounds they might hear in the country. Let them each share sounds they like or dislike in each setting.

• Ask the children to sit very quietly, close their eyes, and listen to the sounds they hear around them, such as the hum of the lights, a passing car, the clock ticking, coughing, water dripping, and so on. Discuss what they hear.

• Teach the first verse of the Theme Song, "We Can Hear."

◆ **Acting Justly.** Talk with the children about how grateful we should be for the gift of hearing that God has given us. Suggest that they take a few moments at the end of each day to think about all the sounds they heard that day. Encourage them to offer a prayer of thanks each night before they go to bed for the wonderful gift of hearing that God has given them.

◆ **Praying Together.** Invite the children to pray after you: "Dear God, we thank you for the many sounds we hear each day. Amen."

How would your life be different if you could not hear?

God, we thank you for letting us hear the sounds around us. Help us to listen to one another.

Day 2

◆ **Gathering Together.** Be sensitive to hearing-impaired children and adapt this session accordingly. Begin by singing the first verse of the Theme Song, "We Can Hear." Have a music box playing as the children assemble. Invite them to close their eyes and to listen with all their attention to the beautiful sound of the music box playing. Lead them to a sense of awe and wonder at the delicate tones of the music.

◆ **Sharing Together.** Talk with the children about sounds heard in a city. Tell the children that today you would like to share a story with them about sounds that are very different from the music they have just heard. Explain that the story is about sounds heard in the city. Then invite the children to suggest what some of those sounds might be. List these on the chalkboard. Let the children demonstrate some of these sounds. Allow this to be a fun activity for them.

• Have the children open their books to pages 92 and 93. Read the story with great expression. Use gestures where possible and pause at the rebus drawings. Have the children call out the words and sounds for the drawings as you go along. Enjoy!

• Talk about sounds heard in the country. If the children are from a rural area, ask them to share some of the sounds they hear. Show a picture of a farm or ranch and talk about some of the sounds heard in those places. Allow each child time to contribute to the discussion.

• Play a guessing game. Give each child a sheet of drawing paper and have them fold it in half. On one side let them draw a picture of something that makes a sound heard in the city; on the other, something that makes a sound heard in the country. Invite the children to come up one at a time, hold their picture behind them, and make the sound of whatever they have drawn. See if the group can guess what they have drawn from the sound. Then have the child show the picture.

◆ **Acting Justly.** Talk with the children about the wonder of the gift of hearing. Ask how they can show they are grateful for this gift. Challenge them to listen as carefully as possible to the sounds around them for the rest of the day and to be ready to come to the next session and tell if they heard something they never noticed before. Ask them to notice sounds that call them to help someone or something.

◆ **Praying Together.** Gather in the prayer center. If the music box melody is appropriate, you may wish to play it in the background as you pray. Lead the children in a simple prayer asking God to help them to listen well. For example: "Loving God, thank you for the gift of hearing you have given us. Help us to listen carefully to all the wonderful sounds in our world." Have the children respond together, "Amen."

Day 3

◆ **Gathering Together.**   Begin by singing the first verse of the Theme Song, "We Can Hear." Invite the children to share any sounds they heard since the previous session that they had never noticed before. Ask them about sounds that called them to help someone. Share with them some of the sounds you have heard. Then explain that today they will learn about a wonderful way in which parts of our bodies work together when we hear sounds.

◆ **Sharing Together.**   On the chalkboard draw a stick figure of a person on which the person's ears and heart are evident. Print the word *sounds* with an arrow pointing to the ears and the word *feelings* with an arrow pointing to the heart. Explain that in today's lesson they will see that there is a very close connection between the sounds we hear and the things we feel. Draw an arrow between these two words on the chalkboard.

• Invite the children to open their books to pages 94 and 95. Read the first two sentences. Ask if they can tell from the picture if Jared is in a city or in the country. Have them point out some things that would tell he is in a city, such as sidewalks, fire hydrants, trash cans, paved streets, and so on. Explain that the sounds that Jared hears from his window might not be the same sounds they would hear from theirs. Invite them to draw something Jared might see from their windows that would make a sound. Finish reading page 94 and do the suggested activity.

• Think about sad and happy sounds. Have the children look at the picture on pages 94 and 95. Read page 95 and ask them to name as many happy and sad sounds as they can. List these on the chalkboard. Explain that we call these happy or sad sounds because of the connection they have with our feelings. Lead them to see that our words can make people feel happy or sad.

Show a picture of children conversing. Ask what one child might say to the other that would make him or her feel happy. For example: "You're pretty" or "How smart you are" or "Thanks for helping me." Do the same with words that might make others feel sad. For example: "You're no fun" or "You are so dumb!"

◆ **Acting Justly.**   Talk with the children about how they can change sad sounds into happy ones by helping people. Ask them to be alert to ways they could do this for the rest of the day.

◆ **Praying Together.**   Gather around the prayer table. Invite the children to join hands as you lead them in this prayer: "Lord, thank you for the power you have given us to change sad words into happy ones. Thank you for making us so wonderful. Teach us to speak words that will always make others happy and not sad." Have all the children respond, "Amen."

What do you most enjoy listening to in life?

How do you change angry words into happy ones?

Our willingness to listen can greatly influence the happiness of another. Who really listens to you?

Day 4

◆ **Gathering Together.** Begin by singing together the first verse of the Theme Song, "We Can Hear." Recall what the children have learned this week about the wonderful gift of hearing and the many varied sounds in our world God has given us.

◆ **Sharing Together.** If possible, obtain some small instruments, such as a triangle, bells, sticks, a tambourine, clappers, a drum, and so on that the children can use to make sounds. If a piano or guitar is available and someone can play either instrument, use it by all means. Let the children use the instruments and notice the beautiful sounds that each one makes. Have them also appreciate how one sound can complement another.

Hum or sing a simple melody, such as "Happy Birthday" or "Jingle Bells," or play the melody on the piano or guitar. Have the children accompany the music with their instruments. Allow them time to experience the joy of working together to make this music.

> *OPTIONAL:* Listen to a recording of an orchestra together. Play a small portion of a beautiful orchestra piece. Have the children listen carefully to see how many instruments they can identify. Ask them how the music makes them feel.

◆ **Acting Justly.** Give each child a cutout of an outline of a child's head on which ears and a mouth have been drawn. Invite the children to print on one ear a sound they like to hear, such as bells, a dog barking, someone singing, hands clapping, and so on. On the other ear, ask them to print a happy word or words, such as "Hello," "Thank you," "Good!" and so on. On the mouth, have them print a word or words they will say to make someone feel happy, such as "Please," "I'm sorry," "Play with me," and so on. Join with them in doing this writing exercise and share with them what you have written. Encourage the children to try always to speak kind words.

◆ **Praying Together.** Have the children gather in the prayer center with the cutouts they have produced. Invite them to stand in a circle around the table for the prayer service. Lead them in the prayer on page 96. Follow the annotations as a guide.

WE LISTEN TO STORIES ABOUT JESUS

God's Word

God often spoke to the people of the Bible through prophets and preachers.
✍

How well do you listen to the words of Scripture read at Mass?
✍

Journeying in Faith

The Bible is a book; actually, a collection of books. But before it became a book, it was a story that people told, the story of God's great works for the people of Israel.

The words of the Bible were heard before they were read. The principal stories of the Bible were about special people: what they did and what they said. The great persons in the Bible, from Moses to Jesus, were teachers and preachers who spoke through their deeds. When they preached, people listened. When they acted, people told stories about what they had done. The word was heard as a challenging word before it was ever written.

It was a word addressed to communities as a whole and to individuals within the communities. Some communities listened and responded to the challenge of the word. Others did not listen or did not accept the challenge because it was forgotten or not heard.

Two stories in the Jewish Scriptures (the Old Testament) tell us about the importance of both the proclaimed word and a listening people in the life of the community. The first is the story of Deuteronomy and the second is the story of Ezra.

In the seventh century before Christ, the Assyrians had forced the Jews to abandon many of their traditional religious practices. The Jews even allowed the Temple built by Solomon to fall into ruin. A young Israelite king named Josiah decided to rebuild the Temple. In the course of the reconstruction, the workmen rediscovered the "Book of the Law of the Lord," that is, Deuteronomy.

One of the secretaries read the "Book of the Law" aloud to Josiah. The king listened and then realized how far God's people had drifted from keeping the covenant God had made with them. Josiah gathered together the leaders of Judah and all the inhabitants of Jerusalem, "the whole population, high and low." He called them to listen as the Book of the Law was read to them. Listening to the words brought the people to recognize their unfaithfulness. The proclamation and acceptance of the word marked the beginning of a religious revival in Judah.

Two centuries later, the Babylonians sacked Jerusalem, destroyed the Temple, and carried the Jewish leaders with some of their people into exile. Many of the Jews turned away from God and, again, worshiped false idols. Later the Persians conquered the Babylonians, and they allowed the Jews to return to their homeland. The Jews went home with weakened faith.

The people said of Jesus' message, "This is a hard word." Do you agree?

How do you respond when you hear Jesus' words?

On their return, the Jews began to rebuild the city and the Temple. But even with these works going on, they realized they needed a stronger faith to sustain them in difficult times. If Yahweh was to bless and protect them, they needed to reaffirm their faith-covenant. On the great feasts of tents, the people gathered together, men, women and children old enough to understand. They called on Ezra, a priest and scribe, to bring forth the Book of the Law of Moses and to proclaim it to them. Ezra read aloud from early morning until noon. The people listened. They listened to the word, took it to their hearts, and it led them back to the Lord God.

Jesus also was a preacher. He proclaimed God's word to his people. Some listened and became his disciples. Others listened and turned away, saying, "This is a hard word." How would you have responded to hearing Jesus' words?

After the resurrection, the apostles proclaimed the "good news" to the people assembled in Jerusalem for the celebration of Pentecost. Visitors from all over the world heard the message, "each in his own native language" (Acts 2:8). People listened and responded. Many were baptized as a result.

Later, the good news of Jesus was fleshed out with more detail. Some followers began to collect the sayings of Jesus. The story of the Last Supper and his passion and death were told as the people gathered for the breaking of the bread. The first of the gospels as we know them, the gospel of Mark, was completed about twenty-five years after Jesus' death-resurrection. Up to that time, the Church had depended on word of mouth to keep Jesus' sayings alive.

As the first generation of Christians, the disciples who had seen his works and heard him preach, began to die off, the community wanted to preserve these accounts in writing. The gospels according to Mark, Matthew, Luke, and John keep the memory and experience of those first Christians alive.

Christians of the twentieth century listen to the words of scripture, knowing them to echo the words of Christ. Jesus does speak to us and challenge us to accept or reject his word.

WE LISTEN TO STORIES ABOUT JESUS

God's Word

Journeying in Faith with Children

Aims

- To identify storytellers
- To appreciate that the disciples of Jesus were good storytellers
- To listen again to stories we have heard about Jesus and to review what they teach us

New Words

storyteller
disciples

Materials

Day 1: • photos of family
         storytellers
       • Bible
       • drawing materials
Day 2 • Bible
       • drawing materials
Day 3 • name cards: Matthew,
         Mark, Luke, John,
         Gospel, Good News
       • drawing materials
       • Bible
Day 4 • red construction paper
         and scissors

Theme Song

"We Can Hear" from the cassette *Songs for Living Waters 1* by Stephen Chapin

Day 1

◆ **Gathering Together.** Begin by singing the first verse of the Theme Song, "We Can Hear." Have the children open their books to page 97. Ask them to look carefully at the picture and to tell what they think is happening. Have them notice that the children in the picture are listening to the boy who has his arms stretched out. Ask what they think he is doing. Lead them to see that he is telling a story.

◆ **Sharing Together.** Ask the first question on page 97. Have the children give reasons why they like to listen to stories. Explain that both children and adults love stories. Have them look at the picture again to see if they think the children in the picture look interested in the story the boy is telling. Have them tell how they know.

Explain to the children that storytelling has always been an important part of people's lives, but it was especially important before books came to be written. The only way that people could remember the important things that had happened in their lives was to pass them on from one family member to another by telling stories.

• Read page 97 to the group and invite the children to respond to the remaining questions. Share with them some stories your own family has passed on through the years. If you have photos of any of your family storytellers, show them to the children. Tell them what it is that makes him or her a good teller of stories.

• Show the children a Bible. Explain that after Jesus' death and resurrection, his friends shared stories about him. Everywhere they went they gathered people together and told them stories about all the wonderful things Jesus had done. We call these friends Jesus' disciples.

◆ **Acting Justly.** Give each child a sheet of drawing paper. Tell the children to pretend they are disciples. Invite them to think of a story about Jesus that they can tell to others. Ask them to draw a picture to help them tell the story. Have them share their stories with the group. Encourage them to tell their stories about Jesus to their family and friends. Ask them how they can act like Jesus.

◆ **Praying Together.** Gather the children in the prayer center. Have them repeat this prayer after you: "O God, we thank you for all the storytellers in our lives. Help us to listen to them. Amen."

Day 2

◆ **Gathering Together.** Gather in the sharing center. Begin by singing the first verse of the Theme Song, "We Can Hear." Review what they have learned about being storytellers.

Ask the children whether they like to share with others when something has happened to them for which they are proud, such as receiving good grades in school, making something for one of their parents, receiving an award for something that they have done well, and so on. Comment on what good storytellers they are becoming.

Review with the children the meaning of the word *disciples*. Ask if any of them know how the disciples became followers of Jesus. Have as many children as possible respond.

◆ **Sharing Together.** Have the children turn to pages 98 and 99 in their books and examine the picture. Let them take time to enjoy the picture and to comment on it. Have them notice the water seems rough and the man's hair is blowing in the wind. Ask the children: What are the men doing? Have you ever seen the nets people use to fish? Ask if they know who the men in the picture are. Point out that these first followers of Jesus were ordinary working men.

Read the story on pages 98 and 99 to the group. Reflect on the fact that people must have wondered how these men became followers of Jesus.

Point out that one of the first stories about Jesus that the disciples shared with some of their friends was how Jesus had called them from among all the other people. They were probably proud to have been called.

Tell the story of how Jesus called the disciples and have the children use simple gestures to dramatize it. Place your text inside the Bible when reading it to demonstrate to the children that the story comes from the Bible. After the dramatization, have the children tell what their feelings were.

◆ **Acting Justly.** Invite the children to become followers of Jesus and to tell stories to others about Jesus as the first disciples did. Have them draw a picture of a story about Jesus that they will share with someone.

◆ **Praying Together.** Gather the children around the prayer table. Ask them to close their eyes and listen quietly as you lead them in the following prayer. Have them say the words after you: "Jesus, we want to be your disciples, too. Help us to know and love you better. Help us to share stories about you with others. Amen."

What are the stories your family retells as part of its family history?

Are you a good storyteller? Do people listen when you tell stories?

Day 3

◆ **Gathering Together.** Begin by singing the Theme Song, "We Can Hear." Invite the children to pretend that they are among the first disciples of Jesus and that they want people to know about Jesus. Play a game with them called "Passing on the Good News." Have the children form into two lines with one person behind the other. Whisper a message about Jesus into the ear of the first person in each line. Give each line a different message. Each child should quietly pass on the message to the next person in line. The last person in each line should announce the message aloud to the whole group.

◆ **Sharing Together.** Explain that something like this happened after Jesus' resurrection. Using name cards, explain that Matthew, Mark, Luke, and John knew that the story of Jesus was very important. They wanted everybody to remember it. Each one decided to write down what he had heard about Jesus. Each one told many of the same stories but each told it in his own way. These biblical stories about Jesus are called the gospels. Explain that the word *Gospel* means "Good News."

• Have the children turn to pages 100 and 101 in their books. Read the stories about Jesus to them from their books. Ask why it helps to have Jesus' stories written down.

Ask the children what their favorite story about Jesus is. Give each child a sheet of drawing paper and have them draw a picture of the story, putting themselves into it. Then have them share with the group the story they have chosen and tell what they imagined themselves doing in the story.

◆ **Acting Justly.** Suggest that the children encourage their parents to read the Bible to them during the week. Invite them to promise Jesus that they will listen attentively to learn as much as they can about Jesus.

◆ **Praying Together.** Move to the prayer center. Invite the children to stand around a table on which the Bible has been placed. Have each child come up, place his or her drawing on the table, and pray, "Jesus, I love you and want to be your follower." Lead the group in prayer by saying, "Help us to listen to your stories and to share them with everyone we meet." Everyone answers, "Amen."

Remember how Jesus loved the little children and listened to them carefully. Do you really listen to them?

What can you do to tell the stories of Jesus so that the children will listen well?

Day 4

◆ **Gathering Together.** Begin by gathering the children in the sharing space. Sing the first verse of the Theme Song, "We Can Hear."

◆ **Sharing Together.** Divide the children into three groups. Ask the first group to look at page 97, the second group at pages 98 and 99, and the third group at pages 100 and 101. Ask each group to share with the whole group everything they remember learning about the pictures they see there.

• Help them to recall the importance of storytelling, that Jesus was a great storyteller, and that Jesus' disciples told stories about him. Help them remember the call of the disciples and how these disciples wrote down stories about Jesus.

◆ **Acting Justly.** Remind the children that Jesus wants us to carry on his work and do the things he would do if he were living here today. Ask each child to offer one suggestion about what Jesus might want them to do. Give each child a sheet of red construction paper and have the children cut out a heart. Have them print on one side of the heart what they will do to show that they want to be like Jesus. On the other side, have them print their names. Ask the children to bring their hearts to the prayer center.

◆ **Praying Together.** Gather the children together in the prayer center. Lead the children in the prayer service on page 102, using the reading on page 44 from Luke about Jesus blessing the children. Bless the children as recommended in the annotations.

May the Holy Spirit empower us to listen to the stories of Jesus.

PART THREE
WE LISTEN TO JESUS' TEACHINGS

The Church

Words are not heard until we let them enter into our hearts. What do you think this means?

✍

Why is it "risky" to listen to Jesus' words?

✍

Journeying in Faith

After experiencing Jesus' life, death, resurrection, and the coming of the Spirit, the followers of Jesus shared the good news they had received by preaching this good news to others. The first converts to Christianity came from those who listened to this preaching.

The written gospels contain evidence that they were first an oral proclamation. There is a certain rhythm in many passages that is characteristic of an oral rather than a literary style. Also, there are certain techniques used to facilitate memory, such as repetition, rhymes, alliteration, grouping in numbers, and connecting catchwords. The good news was proclaimed, listened to, and then accepted or rejected by the listeners.

The gospels are filled with the words of Jesus. In Jesus' last discourse with the disciples, he says to them and to us, "I call you friends, because I have told you everything I heard from my Father" (John 15:15).

"And you are my friends," Jesus says, "if you do what I command you" (John 15:14). What command does he give us? "My commandment is this: love one another just as I love you" (John 15:12). Are we listening as the words of Christ are proclaimed? Do we really hear them?

We have heard his words countless times. They are proclaimed in the gospel, echoed in preaching, and are a prominent theme in Christian teaching. Sometimes we speak them to others. Still many of us are like Jesus' listeners who had ears but did not hear.

Hearing is an active listening. Words are not heard until we let them enter into our hearts. When we hear, we open ourselves to the word and allow it to transform us, to become part of us. Openness to the words of Jesus is risky. Once we open ourselves to his word, our lives will be changed. Often we do not hear because we will not risk such change.

Who are those "others" whom Jesus commands us to love? To whom must we extend our friendship? In the Sermon on the Mount, Christ was quite specific about this. He said that we are to love our enemies and pray for persecutors. If enemies and persecutors are to be included in our love, then so must everyone else be included. The Christian commandment of love is totally inclusive. No man, woman, or child may be excluded.

Why is listening an expression of love?

Christian love extends to everyone, but it begins in the home. It begins with the husband listening to and loving his wife and the wife her husband. Both husband and wife are to listen to and love their children, and the children are to listen to and love their mother and father and one another. If we do not listen to one another, love cannot be a reality in the family.

How is love shown? If we listen to the word of Paul, one of the greatest Christian preachers, we will know. St. Paul, in his letter to the Corinthians, describes love as patient and kind. Love is not jealous, does not put on airs, is not snobbish, is never rude, is not self-seeking, and is not prone to anger. Love does not brood over injuries nor rejoice in what is wrong. There is no limit to love's forbearance, to its trust, its hope, and its power to endure.

The Christian commandment of love is totally inclusive. Do you believe this? What difference does it make in your life?

Is it possible to love in this way? It is possible if we recognize that we, ourselves, are loved in this way. Jesus has called us friends and made known to us all that he heard from the Father. He told us that the Father loves us and we are to love one another. Jesus tells us that we are loved with a love that is patient, kind, unselfish, limitless. This love poured out on us enables us to love others. Jesus listened to the Father. Are we listening to Jesus?

At Mass each Sunday, we pray, "Lord, hear my prayer." We ought also to pray, "Lord, help me to hear your word." One word that Jesus gave us as commandment is the word to love one another. We can tell if we are hearers of the word by looking at our own lives and seeing if our actions are ones of love and service for all people.

WE LISTEN TO JESUS' TEACHINGS

The Church

Journeying in Faith with Children

Aims

- To appreciate that good friends listen to one another
- To learn that we listen to Jesus' teaching when the gospels are read
- To listen to Jesus' teaching on the Great Commandment

New Words

peacemaker   listen

Materials

Day 1: • pictures of a home scene, a school, children playing, and people talking
- a short story or rhyme to read to the children
- Bible

Day 2: • large sheet of newsprint
- marker
- drawing paper
- crayons

Day 3: • none

Day 4: • construction paper
- scissors
- crayons and other craft materials

Theme Song

"We Can Hear" from the cassette *Songs for Living Waters 1* by Stephen Chapin

Day 1

◆ **Gathering Together.** Remind the children that some people cannot hear but they can communicate by using sign language, or signing. Review any signing you may have taught. Sing the first verse of the Theme Song, "We Can Hear."

Talk about listening. Print L _ _ _ _ _ on the chalkboard. Remind the children about a wonderful gift God has given to each of us, the gift of hearing, or listening. Call on a volunteer to come and complete the word on the chalkboard that tells what God wants us to do with our ears.

◆ **Sharing Together.** Have the children open their books to page 103. Lead them in a discussion of the picture by asking the first question. Then use pictures of a home scene, a school scene, children playing, and people talking to illustrate the material on this page.

• Read a very short story or a rhyme to the children. Ask them to listen closely and try to remember as much of the reading as they can. When finished, invite them to tell one thing they remember about the story or rhyme. Compliment them on being good listeners.

◆ **Acting Justly.** Talk with the children about things that they can do to become better listeners. Suggest that they try to become very quiet inside. They should try to pay attention by looking at the person who is speaking. They should not interrupt someone who is speaking.

Encourage the children to do what they can this week to become better listeners. Perhaps they could choose one of the things they suggested and work on it each week during the coming month. Ask them to practice listening at home.

◆ **Praying Together.** Invite the children to join hands and form a semicircle around you. Read to them a short verse or part of a psalm from the Bible. Pause after each verse and have all the children respond: "Help us, O Lord, to hear your word." When finished, end with this prayer: "Lord, we thank you for letting us hear your word. Help us now to go out and live it." Have all the children respond, "Amen."

What are some things in your life that impede you from really listening to others?

God, our Father, thank you for the gift of our ears.

Day 2

◆ **Gathering Together.** Begin by singing the first verse of the Theme Song, "We Can Hear." Mount a large sheet of newsprint with the words *Good News* printed at the top. Explain that today we will hear some of the wonderful things Jesus taught. Ask the children to raise their hands if they hear something they think is good news as you read to them. Print their contributions on the newsprint as you go along.

◆ **Sharing Together.** Invite the children to become very quiet both outwardly and within themselves so that they can better listen to Jesus' words. Have them turn to pages 104–105 in their books and notice how the people are listening to Jesus. Read the first sentence on page 104 and the words of Jesus that follow it, slowly and emphatically. If no one raises a hand, pause and ask the children if they heard any good news in what you read. Write on the newsprint or the chalkboard the words *Jesus is our friend.* Explain that Jesus' friends do what he asks.

Invite the children to stand. Read the first line of the second paragraph, "Friends listen to each other." Have the children read together with you the remaining four statements on page 104.

◆ **Acting Justly.** Read page 105 slowly and emphatically. Have the children read Jesus' words aloud with you. Then focus on the two questions. Encourage the children to suggest ways they will try to be peacemakers for family and friends.

• Teach the second verse of the Theme Song, "We Can Hear."

Help the children discover and appreciate that we are friends of Jesus. Distribute sheets of drawing paper. Have each child draw a picture of one scene that shows how a friend of Jesus would act in a situation today. After all have finished, gather the pictures and mix them up. Have each child pick out one drawing from the pile. The child who did the drawing should explain what it represents; the child who chose it should be encouraged to try to live out that way of being a friend of Jesus during the coming week. Try to motivate the child who did the drawing to allow the person who chose it to take it home as a reminder of what she or he will try to do.

◆ **Praying Together.** Place the textbook opened to pages 104–105 on the prayer table. Have the children gather around the table in a circle and hold hands. Lead your group in this prayer: "O God, we praise you for giving us Jesus as a friend. Help us to act as a friend to others. Amen." Have the children repeat the words of the prayer after you.

Day 3

◆ **Gathering Together.** Begin by gathering the children and singing the first two verses of the Theme Song, "We Can Hear." Remind the children that Jesus asked us all to be peacemakers. Discuss how we can be peacemakers at home and in school. Have the children open their books to page 106. Ask them to listen carefully while you read the page aloud. Then invite them to read it together with you. Have one child ask the opening question. Read the narrated parts yourself and invite all the children to read Jesus' words together. Call attention to the illustrations. Encourage the children to enjoy them and to tell what is happening in each.

◆ **Sharing Together.** Explain to the children that the words of Jesus on page 106 are only half of Jesus' answer. Have them look at page 107 to find the other half of Jesus' words and read them together. Point out that Jesus asked us to do these two things. These words of Jesus are called the Great Commandment. Have the children repeat the two parts of the Great Commandment together.

• Teach the third verse of the Theme Song, "We Can Hear."

◆ **Acting Justly.** Ask the children to name some people in their families, parish, or neighborhood who might be "neighbors" in need. These neighbors might be parishoners who are poor, a parent who is not feeling well, a brother or sister who needs help with homework, or a new child who has moved into the neighborhood and has no friends. Ask them to pretend they are listening to each of these people and to imagine how they would want to be loved. Invite them to share their responses with one another. Emphasize that we need to listen to people so that we can be of help when we are needed. Encourage the children to respond to people in need in loving ways.

◆ **Praying Together.** Gather in the prayer center. Have the children quiet themselves. Then lead them in a litany for those in need. Have them respond to each of the petitions with the words, "Lord, we pray."

Catechist: O God, we ask your help,
                For those in need . . .
                For those who are lonely . . .
                For those who are sick . . .
                For those who are poor . . .
                For those who are hungry . . .
                For all those who need our help . . .

                We thank you, God, for listening to our prayer.

All: Amen.

What does it really mean to listen to Jesus?

Who needs your help today?

Help the children imagine how those in need would like to be listened to.

Day 4

◆ **Gathering Together.** Begin by singing all the verses of the Theme Song, "We Can Hear." Ask the children to listen carefully and then read aloud the Great Commandment. Ask the children why it is important to listen to stories about what Jesus said and did. Ask why we call these stories Good News. Call for responses to the questions: What other stories of Jesus have you listened to? How are they Good News?

◆ **Sharing Together.** Review the story of the Good Samaritan for the children (pages 70–71). Remind them that Jesus told this story when someone asked, "Who is my neighbor?" Have the children talk about what Jesus is telling people who listen to the story of the Good Samaritan.

◆ **Acting Justly.** If we are listening to Jesus, we ought to help someone in need. Have the children tell about someone in their neighborhood or school who may be in need. You may wish to use some examples from the previous day's lesson. Share with them any stories that you may know about persons in need. Ask the children to listen carefully to all the stories so we can decide what to do.

Decide on a group project and have all the children work on it together. You might have the children make place mats for elderly persons in a nursing home. These might be made of construction paper and decorated with shells or beads glued to them. Or you might have the children make a get-well card for someone in the school or parish who is sick.

◆ **Praying Together.** Invite the children to form a prayer circle and lead them in praying the prayer on page 108. Follow the annotations as marked for leading the prayer.

PART FOUR
WE LISTEN AT MASS

We Pray

The Lord asks us only to open ourselves to the word addressed to us. What do you need to do to really hear God's word to you?

✍️

How does the silence at Mass help you to accept God's word?

✍️

Journeying in Faith

How many words do you hear each day? each month? each year? We hear thousands of words each week. Some of these words are trivia, some are a medium of human exchange, a few are very special, and these few, which we shall call "the great words," change our lives.

Great words are memorable. They affect us deeply. When we hear them, we are affected by them. When we remember them, the feeling we had when we first heard them returns. Through them the speaker is in some way present to us. Sometimes we write down these "great words" because they are so precious to us.

The Christian community also treasures its great words. It preserves them in writing and it hands them on by gathering the community together to hear them. The Bible is called Sacred Scripture, or holy writings, because the community accepts it as the word of God addressed to it. The books of the Bible were written and preserved by earlier communities as a testimony to God's action in the lives of his people. This people formed by God was inspired to share God's presence through this word.

Christ "is present in his word, since it is he himself who speaks when the holy Scriptures are read in the church," says Vatican II. The word of Scripture is not just a word about a glorious past. It is a word addressed to us today. Jesus is present in his word calling us as the people of God in the past were called to respond. The word is spoken to us as a great word, a word that invites us to accept it into our lives.

Whenever we celebrate any of the sacraments, we begin with a liturgy of the word. The Church proclaims the word because it is a word in which God reveals God's self to us and calls us to respond to God. It is an affective word. It will change us if we are open to it. We must listen to it if we are to hear it.

The liturgy of the word is structured in such a way that it alternates between address and response. It is like a good conversation between friends in which one listens and then replies to what has been said. In the

The homily breaks open the bread of the word so that all might share it. What do you think are some characteristics of a good homily?

When we become good listeners, the word is able to take root in our lives. It should make a difference. Does it?

liturgy of the word, God begins the conversation and asks us only to open ourselves to the word addressed to us.

The liturgy of the word at the Sunday Eucharist shows the pattern of the service. It begins with a reading from the Jewish Scriptures. After hearing the word from the Jewish Scriptures, we need time for silence, a silence that will enable us to absorb the word we have heard. That word was not a superficial word but a communication from God. We need silence if the word is to penetrate our hearts.

Following the silence, we speak as a community. We respond to the word which we have heard. The responsorial psalm is our way of saying, "Yes, Lord!" to the word which we have heard.

The rhythm of address and response continues. The word in the second reading from the epistles frequently develops a different theme, but it, too, summons us to remember who we are and to recognize the Lord in the word that is proclaimed. As a great word, it stirs up faith and nourishes us, so that we can go forth and live out this faith. We are grateful for this word, and we respond to it, "Thanks be to God."

Again silence. We need time to take in the word that has been uttered. This silence is not empty. It is creative time in which meaning and life come together so that new meaning and new life can be born.

The liturgy moves on, and we stand in anticipation to prepare ourselves to hear the gospel. "Alleluia!" we sing. "Alleluia! Praise Yahweh!" We praise before we hear the gospel for we know that this word is the word of Christ. Through this word, Christ is present to us. In this word, Christ summons us to be his disciples. In response, we say, "Praise to you, Lord Jesus Christ!"

The homily or sermon that follows explains the word heard in the readings and is itself an integral part of the liturgy of the word. The homily breaks open the bread of the word so that all might share it. A homily is not an accidental part of the Mass that may or may not be included. Something important is missing when there is no homily. It is a response to the readings. In the homily, the preacher responds to the word that all or us have heard and calls on all of us to respond.

In the Sunday liturgy, we sum up our reply to the word that we have heard with our profession of faith. We stand again and renew our baptism through the proclamation of the creed. The word we have heard has led us to this. We proclaim that we believe. We believe in the God who has spoken to us.

The liturgy of the word is followed by the Prayer of the Faithful. In this prayer, the Church intercedes for the world and we pray for those in need. We call on the Father whom we have heard and beseech God to hear our prayer. Moved by God's word, we ask God to care for the Church and the world that the Creator has brought into being.

We Pray

Journeying in Faith with Children

Aims

- To reflect on what it means to listen carefully
- To learn to be a good listener when the Bible is read at Mass
- To learn the responses to the readings at Mass
- To discover that God listens to our prayers

New Words

Word of God
obey

Materials

Day 1: • picture of a young boy or girl
  • badges
Day 2: • Bible
  • candle
Day 3: • name card: Praise to you, Lord Jesus Christ.
Day 4: • five large cards
  • strips of colored construction paper
  • pencils
  • stapler
  • bowl of water for prayer

Theme Song

"We Can Hear" from the cassette *Songs for Living Waters 1* by Stephen Chapin

Day 1

◆ **Gathering Together.** Begin by singing the Theme Song, "We Can Hear." Show a picture of a young girl or boy about the children's age. Give the child a name and tell the children an imaginary story about the child in the picture. Explain that the child cannot hear. Talk about the many ways this child will attempt to "listen" to people, such as by watching others' lips as they speak or by signing.

Help the children realize how grateful we should be for the wonderful gift of hearing God has given us. Point out that one of the better ways of showing our gratitude for this gift is by listening well at all times.

◆ **Sharing Together.** Have the children open their books to page 109 and examine the picture. Ask the two questions at the top of the page and invite as many responses as possible. Have the children talk about the different ways the children in the picture on the page are listening. Ask what story the man might be reading, what TV program the children might be watching, and so on.

• Reflect with the children on ways we listen during prayer. Ask the children whether they think that some things might be more important to listen to than others. Have them look at the title of the lesson on page 109. Ask why it is especially important to listen at Mass. Lead them to see that God speaks to us during Mass and that it is important that we listen.

◆ **Acting Justly.** Ask the children if they would like to make a promise to listen well, now that they have learned how important it is. Have a simple promise ceremony. Let the children place their left hands over their ears and raise their right hands as they say together: "I pledge to listen well when others speak. I promise to listen to God's Word at Mass." Make badges to present to the children when they report about something they heard because of listening well. The badges could say "I listen well."

◆ **Praying Together.** Gather the children together and invite them to reflect quietly on the wonderful gift of hearing that God has given them. Lead the children in praying: "O God, we praise you and thank you for being able to hear one another. Amen." Pray the words of the prayer aloud and have the children repeat them after you.

When God speaks to you through the Bible, are you listening?

Happy are they who hear the Word of God.

Day 2

◆ **Gathering Together.** Begin by gathering the children and singing all the verses of the Theme Song, "We Can Hear." Ask the children to think about someone they would like to know. Talk with them about how they would do this. Lead them to see that we can get to know a person by listening to what he or she says. We learn by what others say about this person.

◆ **Sharing Together.** Remind the children that when we gather on Sunday and listen to the readings at Mass, we hear what God says to us. We hear what other persons have said about God. Explain that sometimes the words may be a little difficult to understand, but if we listen carefully, we will hear some words we can remember. Tell the children that in today's lesson they will hear a story about a girl to whom this happened.

• Explain to the children that this is a story about a girl named Maria. Read pages 110 and 111 with expression and ask the children to see whether they can discover what important word Maria heard and what important message she received.

On the chalkboard, write "When we hear God's Word and _ _ _ _ it, we are happy." Have a child come up and write in the missing word they heard from listening to the story. Point out that Maria realized what she had done wrong because she was listening well to hear God's Word.

◆ **Acting Justly.** Talk with the children about some ways in which they can obey the Word of God, as Maria did, such as being fair, sharing, helping out at home and school, and so on. Encourage them to choose one of these ways of obeying God and to try very hard during the coming week to do it.

◆ **Praying Together.** Gather the children around the prayer table. Have a Bible and a candle on the table. Lead the children in praying this prayer:

Catechist: Lord, help us to listen to your voice and to obey your Word when we are tempted to be selfish.

Children: Lord, help us to hear your Word.

Catechist: Lord, help us to listen to your voice and to obey your Word when we are tempted to be mean.

Children: Lord, help us to hear your Word.

Catechist: Lord, help us to listen to your voice and to obey your Word when we are tempted to be lazy.

Children: Lord, help us to hear your Word. Amen.

Day 3

◆ **Gathering Together.** Review briefly how the disciples of Jesus passed on the Good News of Jesus to others through the gospels. They decided to write it down so that others wouldn't forget it. Write the word *gospel* on the chalkboard and recall that this is another way of saying "good news."

◆ **Sharing Together.** Ask the children if they have ever noticed what people do at Mass when the priest reads the gospel. Lead them to see that we stand to hear it read because we want to show our respect for and love of the Word of God.

• Have the children examine the picture of the Mass on pages 112 and 113. Read these pages to them. Show the name card showing the gospel response, *Praise to you, Lord Jesus Christ.* Have the children repeat it together. Comment that the members of Maria's parish family were thanking God for hearing the Gospel.

◆ **Acting Justly.** Ask the children whether they think listening well to the Word of God changed Maria in any way. Lead them to see that it had helped her to decide to return the markers she had taken from Bridget. It helped her to realize she must be a more honest person.

Have the children look at the picture of Maria and Bridget on page 113. Ask whether they think it looks like Bridget forgave Maria. Ask how they can tell. Point out the happy expressions on the girls' faces and lead the children to see that listening to and obeying the Word of God brings happiness into our lives. Encourage them to listen to the Word of God when it asks us to forgive others. We obey the Word of God by forgiving anyone who has hurt us and by remembering to ask for forgiveness ourselves.

◆ **Praying Together.** Gather the children for prayer. Begin by singing all the verses of the Theme Song, "We Can Hear." Then lead the children in praying. Have them repeat this prayer response, "Lord, hear our prayer," after each of the petitions.

Cathechist: Lord, help us to be good listeners . . .

Lord, help us to hear and obey your Word . . .

All: Amen.

"Praise to you, Lord Jesus Christ."

We praise Jesus for the wonderful words we hear in the gospel.

We praise God for the gift of hearing.

Day 4

◆ **Gathering Together.** Begin by gathering the children and singing all the verses of the Theme Song, "We Have Ears." Have five large cards ready. On each card write one of the words from this sentence, "We listen to God's Word." Place these cards randomly on your desk and invite five children to come and choose one card each. Explain that each word is part of a sentence that tells something we do during Mass. Ask the five children to arrange the cards in the correct order to make the sentence. Then have the group read the sentence together.

◆ **Sharing Together.** See how much the children can remember about the story of Maria and Bridget. Ask if they can recall what Maria did after she listened to God's Word at Mass. On the chalkboard, print the letters to the word *obey* in incorrect order. Call on a child to come and rewrite the letters in the correct order to spell the word that tells us what Maria did and what we should do after we hear God's Word.

See whether they can remember what Maria did to show she was obeying God's Word. She asked Bridget's forgiveness and also returned what she had taken. Ask the children whether they think this was difficult for Maria to do and have them tell why. Point out that sometimes it takes courage to obey God's Word. We then pray and ask God to give us the strength we need.

◆ **Acting Justly.** Give each child a strip of colored construction paper. Invite each child to write: "I will listen to your Word" on his or her strip. Have each child sign his or her name. Then staple the strips together to make a prayer chain and hang it near the prayer table.

Talk with the children about some ways they might obey God's Word in the coming days. Give them some practical examples of how they can do this at school or at home.

• You may wish to use the *Remembering* pages 115 and 116 to review the chapter to make sure the children see the connections among the four parts of the chapter.

◆ **Praying Together.** Lead the children in praying the prayer on page 114. Practice singing the "Alleluia" before you begin. Have the children look at the prayer and explain that we pray this way at each Mass, and that we often use the words "Lord, hear our prayer." Have the children repeat the words of the response after you a few times. Follow the annotations for leading the prayer service. At the conclusion of the prayer take water and call each child by name and say: "God bless your ears," and so on.

5.
Eyes Are for Seeing

Looking Ahead

How far can you see? Can you see an ant or the moon? In this chapter we will discover what our eyes can do. We cannot see God, but we can see the wonderful things that God has made.

Chapter Aims

OUR LIVES

To discover and appreciate the wonder of our eyes that help us to see

GOD'S WORD

To become aware of and appreciate that we can see what God has made, especially God's greatest gift, people; to learn to take care of all that God has given to us

THE CHURCH

To learn that we can see the Church; the people we see in our parish are the Church

WE PRAY

To become aware of and appreciate all the people we see at Mass who help us to celebrate

---

Chapter Five Theme Song

"Our Eyes" from the cassette *Songs for Living Waters 1* by Stephen Chapin

Using the Chapter Title Page

Invite the children to look with you at the picture on page 117, the Title Page for Chapter Five. The children in the picture are using various instruments to look at something. Ask the children to identify the instrument each child is using and have them suggest what the child might be looking at. Ask if any of them have ever used such things to help them to see.

After reading the chapter title, preview the chapter by reading the "Looking Ahead" box to the children.

Chapter Plan Ahead

Make arrangements for the following items well in advance of the session in which they are used.

• Obtain such items as a magnifying glass, binoculars, a kaleidoscope, telescope, microscope, and a pair of glasses. (Part 1)

• Set up a nature table with a wide variety of things from nature. See the lesson notes for suggestions about what to include on the table. (Part 2)

• Invite members of your parish to join the children for this session. (Part 3)

• Order and preview the suggested audiovisual material. (Part 4)

Audiovisual References

God's Fine Gifts, VHS, Franciscan Communications, 1229 South Santee St., Los Angeles, CA 90015–2566 (Part 4)

Music for the Prayer Services

"We Are Walking in the Light" from the *Hymnal for Catholic Students,* #199.

Our Lives

How would you rate your own ability to really see the world around you?

Do you consider yourself to be sensitive to colors in your environment? In what ways?

Journeying in Faith

"The greatest calamity that could befall a person," says Helen Keller, "is to have sight and fail to see." The ability to see is taken for granted by many of us. We cannot conceive of a sightless existence. Yet often we have eyes and do not see. We are blind to the marvelous colors and shapes that surround us. How would you rate your own ability to really see the world around you?

Open your eyes and look around you! What do you see? The myriad colors of trees, flowers, clouds, blue sky, grass—the wonders of nature. Driving down a city street, we see billboards, automobiles, neon signs, asphalt strips, telephone poles—the constructions of modern society. We live in a world of beauty and ugliness, but we often fail to see our own environment.

We see through our eyes, a marvel of creation. The eye is about an inch across, yet it can see things at a great distance. Through the eye, we see color and a variety of squares, circles, triangles, and trapezoids overlapping and intersecting. With our eyes, we estimate distances. Our eyes protect us from danger, guide us as we move about. Through our eyes, we gain knowledge, absorb the beauty of a painting, and enjoy literature. With our eyes, we see others, our family and friends. With our eyes, we can see ourselves.

The human eye is very sensitive to light. In fact, it cannot see without light. In absolute darkness, we are sightless beings. Even dim or distant light, perhaps the flame of a lighted match, enables us to see. We need light, and the human eye responds and adjusts naturally to the degree of light we have.

As much as we need light, too much light can be blinding. We cannot look directly into the sun. We shade our eyes from its reflected light. We look away from on-coming headlights, and we find glaring light uncomfortable. But we cannot see without light.

The human eye, unlike the eyes of dogs and other animals, can see colors. Color is everywhere. It adds beauty to our lives, attracts our attention, makes our homes and clothes "easy on the eyes." As we see color, not only the eye but the whole person responds. Color influences our disposition, and we describe persons according to our perception of color. We say someone is "blue," or "green with envy." A special day is a "red-letter day." An acquaintance sometimes has "black" moods. No one likes to be called "yellow."

How do artists "see" the extraordinary in the ordinary?

Do you ever catch yourself looking but not seeing? When?

The human eye is truly a wonder. It can overcome tremendous distances to reach its object. Hearing, touch, taste, and smell must come into actual contact with the objects they respond to. The eye can see almost limitless distances, to the stars, which are so far away that their light may have traveled through space for thousands of years.

As wonderful as the human eye is, it is still limited in its vision. And so, we have devised objects to help us see better. Eyeglasses, microscopes, binoculars, telescopes, all expand our vision. Television brings us sights from other lands and cultures and even from outer space. The camera memorializes our vision. It enables us to see again and in a new way the events of our past.

Painters and sculptors are people with particularly sensitive vision. Their eyes are not physically better, but they have trained themselves to see what many of us look at with dulled eyes. They see the extraordinary in the ordinary. They have the power to interpret what they see, so that others can see these ordinary things through the eyes of the artist. Artists help us to see with insight. It has been said of the impressionist painter that he or she paints not the button, but rather the shine on the button. Artists help us to see the shine that glows in all of life.

Seeing is so important a human function that we use sight as a metaphor for intellectual discovery. "I see!" exclaims the youngster while discovering a mathematical relationship. What was hidden is revealed. The concealed is visible.

Why not keep an "eye diary" for one complete day. You will not be able to jot down all that you see, but you will be more conscious of the images before you. Go about and occasionally ask yourself, "What am I really *looking* at now?" Write down what you saw and how you felt when looking at a scene or person.

Once Helen Keller was asked what she missed seeing most of all. She responded, "What I miss most is not being able to see the faces of my family and friends. I long to be able to see how they look and how they show their love and happiness on their faces." Often we who have sight do not really see the faces of family and friends. We are distracted. We look, but we do not really see. What would you miss if you could not see?

PART ONE
WHAT CAN WE SEE?

Journeying in Faith with Children

Our Lives

Aims

- To discover all the wonderful ways that we can see with our eyes
- To recognize things that help us to see better
- To explain that we need light in order to see

New Words

computer	light
magnifying glass	telescope

Materials

Day 1: • crayons
- book of colors
- Bible, candle

Day 2: • objects that help us to see
- duplicated magnifying glass sheets
- crayons and markers
- candle

Day 3: • blindfold
- flashlight and candle
- sheet of tin or heavy aluminum

Day 4: • drawing paper
- crayons
- candle

Theme Song

"Our Eyes" from the cassette *Songs for Living Waters 1* by Stephen Chapin

Day 1

◆ **Gathering Together.** If you can obtain some oversized fun glasses or any toy glasses, such as the kind with the nose attached, put them on as you begin this lesson and chapter.

• An alternative suggestion for beginning the lesson would be to play a game of "I Spy" with your group. Say, "I spy something that is small and round. It has tiny, tiny holes in it. We can open and close our clothing with it. What do I spy?" (A button) "I spy a happy first-grader with a missing front tooth and shiny red hair. Who do I spy?" (Andy)

◆ **Sharing Together.** Have the children turn to the drawing of the computer screen on page 119. Ask them to tell you what different shapes they see, using the questions on the page. Then distribute crayons and have them use their imaginations to make animals from the various shapes. Allow time for sharing.

◆ **Acting Justly.** Encourage the group to become more aware of all the things they see around them. Invite volunteers to describe the color and shape of a favorite toy or pet. Have available a book of colors, which can be obtained at a paint store, to show many of the wonderful colors around us.

Sensitively point out that some people have poor sight or are blind. They communicate by reading braille.

Now direct the discussion to the people whom we see with our eyes. Ask the children what the eyes of people can tell us about them. Then ask, How do your eyes look when you are sick or sad or angry or happy? Encourage the children to tell of ways that they could make sad eyes, happy eyes, angry eyes, and loving eyes.

◆ **Praying Together.** Gather the children around the table in the prayer center and light the candle. Hold a Bible in a reverent manner and tell the group that our Bible contains a prayer thanking God for the wonderful gift of seeing.

Read Proverbs 20:12: "The Lord has given us eyes to see with and ears to listen with." Let the children repeat the simple prayer after you. Then conclude by having everyone say, "Thank you, Jesus, for our wonderful eyes that help us to see all our favorite people and things."

We have the ability to see all the wonders of our world.

What is your favorite part of all that you see in God's creation?

Day 2

◆ **Gathering Together.**   Before you meet for today's session, obtain some of these items: a magnifying glass, binoculars, a kaleidoscope, a telescope, a microscope, and a pair of eyeglasses. This may not be easy, but do try to obtain as many items as you can.

• If you wear eyeglasses, talk about when you first started wearing them and how you first knew you needed them. Emphasize the positive by explaining that eyeglasses help you to see all the wonderful sights in the world, including the children facing you. If a child in your group wears eyeglasses, invite him or her to talk about how they help him or her to see special people and special things.

◆ **Sharing Together.**   Pages 120 and 121 in the child's book show people seeing all kinds of interesting images. Ask the children to identify the things on the pages that help us to see better. Then find out whether they know anyone who uses a microscope or a magnifying glass to see better. Read aloud page 120 up to the directive to tell what is happening in the pictures.

• Now bring out those items that are pictured on page 120. Allow time for the children to look carefully at things through a microscope, magnifying glass, and kalaidescope and tell what happens when they use the item.

• The questions on the bottom of page 120 must be handled with sensitivity. The children may know people who cannot see. If you have obtained a book written in braille for use in Chapter Three, remind the children of it or have it on hand. Emphasize that those who cannot see with their eyes, "see" with their fingers, hands, and hearts.

• Continue by presenting page 121 and discussing how we can see objects that are faraway. Follow the same procedure as before by asking what is happening in each picture and then going through each example. If you have binoculars or a telescope, show these now to the group. Have the children use these items and look out the window. Ask them to name what they can see and tell how faraway they can see.

◆ **Acting Justly.**   Beforehand, trace an outline of a small magnifying glass on a sheet of paper and duplicate it. Distribute a copy to each child and let the children draw themselves doing something to show to a loved one how much they love and care for that family member or friend. They can be helped to print their names on the glass handle and share their drawings with the selected person. They should do what they have drawn.

◆ **Praying Together.**   Gather the children in a circle in the prayer center. Light the candle and invite the children to pause quietly for a moment to remember all the new things that they have seen today. End by leading the children in praying a simple prayer of thanks, such as: "Dear God, we thank you for all the things and people we can see. Amen."

Day 3

◆ **Gathering Together.** Select a child to be blindfolded. Make this a fun game so that the child does not feel frightened. Lead the child around the room. Stop and ask the child, "Where are you standing?" Tell the child to put a hand on top of his or her head. Then ask the child to touch a toe. Write a numeral on the chalkboard and ask the child to tell what number it is. Lead the group to understand that we can do some things in darkness, such as touching our head or toe, but we need light in order to see things.

◆ **Sharing Together.** Broaden the discussion by asking: "When can you see colors at night? What happens if you take a picture in the dark without a flashbulb? How do the moon and stars help us to see at night?" Help them to see the common element of light in their answers to these questions. The joy of light that helps us to see should be the emphasis here.

• The story on pages 122 and 123 will continue the excitement of this session. Some preparation on your part is needed here. Before meeting with your group for this session, read through the story of the Gomez family as if you are all the characters in the story. Practice with a flashlight and a candle. If possible, get a sheet of aluminum or tin to make the rumbling sounds of thunder.

As you tell the story to your group, dramatize the action. Roll the sheet of aluminum or tin for the rumbling storm, turn your room's light switch on and off for the flash of light, and flicker the lights when appropriate. Sing "Happy Birthday" to Roberto. As the lights go out totally in the Gomez home, turn your room's lights off. Try to get the room as dark as possible by drawing the shades or blocking out the natural light. As the Gomez family copes with the situation, shine the flashlight around the room and light the candle.

All of these actions will help the children see and hear and live the story. If time allows, let them role-play the story and add their own unique touches to the drama.

◆ **Acting Justly.** The questions at the bottom of page 123 allow everyone to share experiences of what helps them see in the dark. Some children may be afraid of the darkness of night. Your emphasizing that light lets us see and do many exciting things is a positive way to deal with any fear of darkness. Let the children share one thing they could do tonight in the light of their homes that would show others how much they love and care for them.

◆ **Praying Together.** Invite the children to the prayer center. Tell them that we are going to praise God for the light that helps us to see. Conduct a simple prayer of praise as you did on the previous day.

What helps you to see better? Think about this carefully.

Every reading in this book can come alive through your creativity and enthusiasm.

We thank God for the gift of light and the gift of eyesight.

Do you know someone who has lost some of his or her sight? How can you help? Is your sight impaired?

Day 4

◆ **Gathering Together.** The children have recognized colors and shapes. They have seen how various instruments help us to see up close and far away, and they have understood how light helps them to see. Hopefully, they are now more appreciative of the priceless gift of seeing all that is in God's creation.

Gather the children around you and let them look for various objects or colors in your room. For example, you might say, "How many red things do you see?" Or you might say, "I see something that is green in our room. What is it?" Emphasize that this week we have seen how our eyes help us to see all the colors and shapes in our wonderful world that God has given us. Be sensitive to children who are color-blind. Let them share what they see.

◆ **Sharing Together.** Have the children cup their hands together in the form of a telescope and give them time to look around the room. Allow time for them to describe how seeing a particular object makes them feel. Let them share how they could use the object to show their love and care for the environment. You may also lead the group to your room's windows to look at various objects in your neighborhood. Again, have them name the objects and have a discussion similar to the preceding one.

◆ **Acting Justly.** Distribute drawing paper and invite the children to draw a picture of those sights that they love to see, especially at night in the light of their homes. This could be an object around the house or a person at home. When all are finished, let the children divide up into pairs. Have one partner tell what he or she sees in the other partner's drawing. Then have the other partner do the same.

Now invite all of the children to share their drawings with the entire group. As each child describes his or her drawing, direct the child to think of one act of love and kindness that he or she could do for the person or object in the drawing. Encourage all the children to actually do the act of love and kindness tonight.

◆ **Praying Together.** Dim your room's lights as you gather the children in the prayer center. Light the candle you have placed on the prayer table. After a moment of stillness, begin the prayer on page 124. Bless the children by making a large Sign of the Cross over them while you say the blessing prayer. Follow the annotations.

WE CAN SEE WHAT GOD HAS MADE

God's Word

What if I knew I would never see something again? How would I feel?

What part of nature causes you to wonder or stand in awe?

Journeying in Faith

Rachel Carson wrote in *The Sense Of Wonder* that "knowledge of our world comes largely through sight, yet we look about with such unseeing eyes that we are partially blind." Our taste and interest have been dulled through overindulgence.

Along with the partial loss of sight has come an inability to wonder. We are in danger of losing our capacity to become excited about things. We tend to take the many gifts of creation for granted. Rachel Carson suggested that you ask yourself, "What if I had never seen this before? What if I knew I would never see it again?" Take a moment to look out the window or around the place in which you are reading these words. Pick out several objects of God's creation and ask yourself these questions.

It may have been the fear of never seeing the beauty of God's world again that prompted Shadrach, Meshach, and Abednego to recite their litany of praise. Sentenced to die in a fiery furnace, the three companions of the prophet Daniel glorified God by singing God's praises. They called up the sun and stars, the mountains, hills and fertile plains, the seas, rivers, and all living things, tame and wild, to bless and exalt the Lord. The book of Genesis looks to God as the source and beginning of the created universe. Most passages in Scripture that deal with creation, however, are concerned with the wonder of God's works. They point to the wonders of creation as evidence of God's greatness. Everything remains in existence only because of God's power and wisdom. The Lord made the earth by his power, established the world by his wisdom, and stretched out the heavens.

In the New Testament, Jesus points to the lilies of the field for an example of God's providence: "Look how the wild flowers grow: they do not work or make clothes for themselves. But I tell you that not even King Solomon with all his wealth had clothes as beautiful as one of these flowers. It is God who clothes the wild grass—grass that is here today and gone tomorrow, burned up in the oven. Won't God be all the more sure to clothe you?" (Matthew 6:28–30)

Think of the many beauties you have seen in your life. Then reread the passage from the gospel of Matthew. How does this make you feel?

One has only to think of some of the natural wonders in our own national parks, such as the Grand Canyon, Niagara Falls, Yosemite National Park, and so on, to stand in awe before the mystery of God's power and wisdom. What part of nature causes you to wonder or stand in awe?

God created all the beauties of the earth. How am I taking care of God's creation?

What can you do to be sure you do not lose your sense of wonder and awe?

God's hand is also evident in more ordinary experiences of everyday life. The author of Proverbs cites an eagle flying in the sky, a snake moving on a rock, a ship finding its way over the sea, and a man and a woman falling love.

Another sage describes the works of the Lord, calling them "the masterpieces of his wisdom." The author says, "All his works are beautiful down to the smallest and faintest spark of light" (Sirach 42:22). Then after listing the great number and variety of God's created works, the wisdom writer concludes: "We could say much more and never finish, but it all means this: the Lord is everything. How can we find the power to praise him? He is greater than all his creation" (Sirach 43:27–28).

But the deeper mystery is that God created all for the use and well-being of humans (Genesis 1:28–30). Too often, this mystery is lost in the hurly-burly of urban living. Commercial exploitation of the world's resources overlooks their beauty. It is naturalists like Rachel Carson who have managed never to lose their sense of wonder and who help us to appreciate the biblical insights. The biblical authors had a poetic vision that permitted them to see into the inner depths of reality. They never tired of contemplating the glory of the created universe or singing the praises of its maker.

PART TWO
WE CAN SEE WHAT GOD HAS MADE

God's Word

Journeying in Faith with Children

Aims

- To see the beauty and wonder in God's creation
- To appreciate the wonders of God's creation
- To praise God for all that God has made
- To recognize that people are the greatest part of God's creation
- To take care of all the things, animals, and people that God has given us

New Words

responsibility
praise

Materials

Day 1: • things from nature
  • nature pictures
  • crayons
Day 2: • photos of the sky and the planets
  • plants, seeds, flowers
Day 3: • photos of water creatures
Day 4: • tray of objects and photos
Use *God's Fine Gifts,* VHS (Franciscan Communications) on Day 4

Theme Song

"Our Eyes" from the cassette *Songs for Living Waters 1* by Stephen Chapin

Day 1

◆ **Gathering Together.**   Set up a table that is overflowing with magazine pictures of plants, nature scenes, animals, and people. Add a beautiful bowl filled with water and flowers, or bring in some plants, seashells, and colorful rocks. A tray of apples, oranges, grapes, and other richly colored fruits and vegetables might also be used to highlight this week's theme. Keep this display of visual delights available to the children throughout the week.

Encourage the children to look at the pictures and touch the items of nature. Allow them to spend some time enjoying the display.

◆ **Sharing Together.**   Direct the group's attention to page 125 in their books. Invite them to guess and then color what is hidden in the lively border illustration.

• The discussion of sometimes not "seeing" what is in our world should be handled in a simple fashion with the first-graders. Explain that because there is so much to see around us that we sometimes forget to really look at and notice all the exciting things and people in our world.

• Teach the first verse of the Theme Song, "Our Eyes."

◆ **Acting Justly.**   Ask for volunteers to tell about some things that they saw on their way to school today. If two or more children came together, let them compare what they saw. Ask why some people notice more things than others. Ask the children to see one thing they can do for others.

◆ **Praying Together.**   Place one or two of the objects of nature that you have obtained on the table in the prayer center. Gather the children around the table and conduct a simple prayer of praise. Praise God for all the wonders of nature that are part of our world.

Catechist: O God, we thank you for all the things
    you have made.
    We thank you for letting us see them.
All: Amen.

God must love us very much to have made so many exciting sights to see.

Everything God made tells us about God. Each thing shows us how wonderful God is.

Day 2

◆ **Gathering Together.** Begin by gathering the children and singing the first verse of the Theme Song, "Our Eyes." Bring in some dramatic photos of a brilliant dawn, the evening sky, the sun, moon, stars, and the planets. Invite the children to think about who put the sun, moon, stars, and planets in our sky.

Add to your table of visual delights by including plants, flowers, seeds, and rocks. Ask the children to name other living and growing things that the children have seen and enjoyed.

◆ **Sharing Together.** Open your book to pages 126 and 127 and read aloud the opening sentence. Emphasize the following to explain the reading:

> "The things God made tell us about God. God made a starry night. God loves me so much to give me a starry night to see. The things God made praise God. When we enjoy a sunny day, we can always thank God for the warmth and goodness we get from the sun.

> "The people and things God made show us how wonderful God is. I love my sister. How wonderful of God to give me a sister."

• As the children share what they can see today and tonight, bring out other examples of what they can see. Tonight, from their bedroom windows, they might see a neighbor's cozy, brightly lighted home or a fire engine racing to help some family in need. Direct the children to your room's windows so that they may share everything that they see. Then ask them to do the same tonight at their home windows with a family member.

◆ **Acting Justly.** Read aloud page 127. Ask the children to point to all the illustrated plants and flowers. Point out that everything that grows and lives in our world shows us how wonderful God is. Explain that this is how creation gives praise to God.

While everyone marks the growing things on the page, ask the question at the bottom. Point out that we must take care of all the things God has made. Ask, "What can you take care of today?" Then have the children share responses.

◆ **Praying Together.** Invite the children to close their eyes and to see, or picture, in their minds all the beautiful growing things that God has made. Pause for a few moments of silence. Ask for a volunteer to stand and mention one of God's gifts. Lead the children to pray in response, "God, you are good and wonderful!" Conclude by prayerfully singing the Theme Song, "Our Eyes."

Day 3

◆ **Gathering Together.**   Begin by singing the first verse of the Theme Song, "Our Eyes." Invite the children to think about a favorite animal that they can pretend to be. Encourage the children to take turns and come up to the front of the room. Have them act out, or pantomime, the animal. Have the other children guess the name of the animal. Then let the child who pantomimed the animal lead the group in thanking God for such a wonderful creature.

◆ **Sharing Together.**   Ask for volunteers to name some creatures who live in lakes, oceans, or rivers. Ask such questions as: Have you ever seen fish or turtles move in the water? Why is it easier for them to live and move in water than it is for us? Help the group to develop a sense of wonder at the many varieties of water creatures that God has given us to see and to protect. Add photos of whales, fish, snails, sharks, starfish, turtles, and so on to your table display of things from nature.

• The appreciation of God's creation continues on page 128 in the child's book. We see the birds and animals, water, and water creatures that give praise to God. Children love to just look at such images, so give enough time for them to enjoy the illustrations on the page. Then talk about how God made all of these sights that make us feel so happy. They show us what God is like.

◆ **Acting Justly.**   Consider the question on page 128 on how to care for the waters that God has made. Help the children to see that when we care for God's creatures in our environment, such as in our back-yards, parks, lakes, and rivers, we show our love both for God and for what God has made.

◆ **Praying Together.**   Place the items you brought in for today's session on the table in the prayer center. Conclude with a short prayer of praise, such as the following:

Catechist: When we see all the birds and animals that God has made, we know,

All: God is good.

Catechist: When we see the oceans and rivers that God has made, we know,

All: God is good.

Catechist: When we see the whales and fish that God has made, we know,

All: God is good.

Catechist: God, help us to care for the waters that show us God is good.

All: Amen.

When we care for and protect our environment, we show our love for all that is in our world. We show our love for God.

How are you caring for the gift of our world?

Think of an experience in your life in which you have been so busy that you missed really seeing.

Day 4

◆ **Gathering Together.**   Ask the children to put their heads on their desks and to close their eyes. Select one of the objects or pictures that you have brought in for this week. Describe its size, shape, usefulness, beauty, color, and so on to the group. Invite the children to guess what you are describing. The first child who guesses correctly then comes to the front of the room and picks up the object or picture for all to see. Continue in the same way with several other objects or pictures.

◆ **Sharing Together.**   Continue exploring the world of God's creation by reading the text and discussing the questions on page 129. Pause for as many answers as possible.

To increase the children's awareness that people are part of God's creation, have them face one another. Ask them to name what they see that can walk, talk, think, and imagine. Help them to see that each person is a part of God's wonderful creation. People are the greatest part of God's creation.

• Teach the second verse of the Theme Song, "Our Eyes."

◆ **Acting Justly.**   Responsibility comes with all the wonderful things that we can do. *Responsibility* is a big word that means that we take care of what God has made. As God's children, we need to show our love for God by being kind and loving to everyone.

You may also want to talk about those people who take care of the whales and save other such endangered species as the bald eagle, those who plant wildflowers near highways, and so on. There are big and small ways that each of us can help take care of what God has made. This is as simple as not dropping candy wrappers and drinking cups on the ground, but disposing of them in wastebaskets. Explain that when we help people to take care of all that God has made, we are praising and thanking God for our wonderful world, which God has given to us to see and enjoy.

◆ **Praying Together.**   The prayer service on page 130 is a fitting closure to this week's session. Follow the annotations in the guide.

WE CAN SEE THE CHURCH

The Church

How would I define the Church?

The Church is a gathering of holy people called together by God. Is this a good definition of your parish community?

Journeying in Faith

What is the Church? Where can we find it? Can we see the Church? The word is first defined in the dictionary as a building for public worship. Another definition presents Church as the whole number of Christian believers or their organized bodies. The dictionary reflects the common understanding of many Christians. First, we see the Church as a building. However, we also recognize that the word is used to describe the whole community of Christian believers.

Before the Church had public buildings, it was known as the Church. This Church is a gathering of holy people called together by God—a community of believers that preaches the gospel, celebrates the eucharist, and is united in love.

Vatican II stated that the Church is a sacrament. It is a symbol or sacrament of Christ. Through the Church, Christ is present in the world today. As a sacrament, it is a visible reality. It makes visible the unseen presence of Christ in the world. If the Church is a visible reality, we should be able to see it. When and where can we see the Church?

The Church is universal, but the Church we see and experience is on the parish or local level. A local congregation is the Church if within it the gospel is preached, the eucharist is celebrated, and it is united in love and service. It is the Church if it is united by the common bond of faith, love, and law with all the other churches.

Each local church is united with the other churches through the bond of the Spirit. This unity is visibly expressed in the college of bishops presided over by the bishop of Rome. As the local church searches for ways to express its life, it seeks verification and testing from the churches. The indivisible Spirit who resides in the churches as one Spirit guarantees the catholicity of the local church.

The Church we can see is a loving Church. It welcomes people of every race and every age. It welcomes the poor and the rich, the sick and the healthy. It includes all those toward whom Jesus showed special care: the blind, the deaf, orphans, widows, and sinners. The Church is visible as a community of people of different nationalities and races, different economic status, different handicaps. If one looks at the Church, one can see men, women, and children of every race and age, who are farmers, clerks, business executives, blue and white collar workers, teachers, secretaries, lawyers, nurses, students.

The Church is a community of believers that preaches the gospel, celebrates the Eucharist, and is united in love and service.

Hopefully, when people look at the Church, they will see a community carrying out Christ's works of mercy. Every parish church should be seen feeding the hungry, clothing the naked, instructing the ignorant, visiting the sick, burying the dead. The Thanksgiving collection of clothes, contributions to the poor, Christmas baskets of food, and support for the missions make visible the serving and caring Church. Catholic hospitals, schools, and social services are also visible expressions of the Church as a serving community.

The Church is not a perfect community. It is a Church in need of purification. It is a pilgrim people on its way, not a people already possessing the fullness of holiness. Sometimes it is seen as prejudiced. Racism and sexism have not been eliminated. The Church proclaims its love for the poor, and yet sometimes it has been seen by the poor as an oppressor. When the Church projects this vision of itself, it is a sign that is unattractive and contradictory.

What are the qualities that best describe my parish?

Bearing witness to Christ's presence in the world is what the Church is meant to do. What the Church bears witness to is seen in its life and actions. If it is seen as joyful and celebratory Church, a reconciling and forgiving community, it bears witness to Christ present within it. A united Church bears witness to its oneness in Christ. A divided Church gives scandal.

What do we see when we look at ourselves as Church? Do we see people of strong faith supporting one another? Do we see a community preaching the gospel and celebrating life with Christ in the eucharist?

What can we do as a local community to be a better sign of the Christ's love?

The Church is a sacrament. It is a visible sign of an invisible reality. What onlookers see when they see the Church leads them to make judgments about it. It is not just the universal Church that is this sacrament. The local parish community is this sacrament. The visible Church is the symbol of the risen Lord present and acting in the world today. Do we, by our lives, make this symbol more opaque or more clearly visible?

PART THREE
WE CAN SEE THE CHURCH

The Church

Aims

- To see all the people who belong to the Church
- To see how the people of the Church serve others
- To see that we are the Church

New Words

Church   lector

pastor   catechist

Materials

Day 1: • collage paper
- drawing paper
- scissors
- paste

Day 2: • drawing paper
- crayons or markers

Day 3: • name card: Church
- drawing paper
- crayons or markers

Day 4: • guest tables
- pencils

Theme Song

"Our Eyes" from the cassette *Songs for Living Waters 1* by Stephen Chapin

Journeying in Faith with Children

Day 1

◆ **Gathering Together.**   Seat the group in a semicircle. Begin by singing two verses of the Theme Song, "Our Eyes." Ask: "What did you see on your way to school today?" "What did you see that you had not seen before?"

◆ **Sharing Together.**   Direct the children's attention to page 131 in their books. Ask for volunteers to look at and name all the people in the picture of the church carnival and picnic. Have them tell what they see happening on the page. Explain that these people are like all the boys and girls and men and women whom we see in our own parish. All these people are the Church.

• Read aloud the banner at the bottom of page 131 that says "Love Truck Benefit." Let the group find the Love Truck in the illustration. Perhaps your parish has a Love Truck. Let them guess what a Love Truck could do to show we are all members of the Church.

◆ **Acting Justly.**   Invite the children to draw or paint a picture of some people they know who belong to your parish. Pin or tape a large sheet of construction paper to a bulletin board or the wall. After the children have drawn one or two parish members, including themselves, help them to cut out the figures and paste them to the piece of construction paper. Title the collage, "We Are _____." Put the name of your parish in the blank space. Do not have a drawing of your church building on this collage. The emphasis here is that the parish members are the Church.

The children may print the initials or the name of the person under the appropriate figure. They should print their names under their own figures. Have the children mention one thing that they could do to help the parish members in the drawing to know that the children love and care for them.

◆ **Praying Together.**   When the collage is completed, gather the children in a semicircle around it. Encourage them to name the people who are the Church in their parish. Then ask each child to name one member of your parish for whom he or she would like to offer a prayer. Have each child pray for the person he or she has named. For example, "I would like to pray for Mrs. Kowalski." The group responds, "Lord, hear our prayer."

121

We can see that the Church is a great family that loves and cares for everyone.

We see the Church when people do caring things for those in need of our love.

Day 2

◆ **Gathering Together.** Begin by gathering the children in the sharing center and having everyone sing the first two verses of the Theme Song, "Our Eyes." Review with the children some of the names of the people who belong to your parish. Have them look at the variety of people who are the Church and tell what ages they see and what nationalities they see. Explain that all the people we see, people of any age and race, are welcome to belong to our family, the Church.

Reinforce the concept that the "Church" is the people whom we see in our parish and all the parishes throughout our world. We are a big family. We care for the needs of one another. We are a family who knows and loves Jesus.

◆ **Sharing Together.** Read pages 132 and 133 together. The drawing on pages 132 and 133 focuses on the Love Truck itself. Continue to emphasize that the people we see in our parish are the Church. They do many things to show that they know and love Jesus. Invite the children to enjoy the illustrations and tell what is happening in each.

◆ **Acting Justly.** Guide the group to understand that the people who are the Church do lots of other things to show that they belong to the Church. There are parish picnics, like the one we just saw, to raise money to help others. We see the Church when the people in our parish do caring things for those who need our help and love.

Ask for volunteers to tell about people they see who do caring and loving things for others. A child may talk about an older brother or sister who is a member of a youth group that visits hospitals and nursing homes to entertain and spread cheer. Another child may have helped his or her parents pack used clothing to give to a family in need.

• Have the children draw pictures of such things as food cartons and boxes of clothing. Add these to the parish collage. They may also draw and paste drawings of parish members helping and cheering up an elderly or sick person. Be sure the children are in the picture, too.

◆ **Praying Together.** Gather the children in the prayer center and lead them in praying a simple prayer, such as the following:

Catechist: The people we see in our parish are the Church.

All: Thank God we can see.

Catechist: We see the Church when we come together for Mass.

All: Thank God we can see.

Catechist: We see the Church when the Church does good things for others.

All: Thank God we can see. Amen.

Day 3

◆ **Gathering Together.**   Begin by singing the first two verses of the Theme Song, "Our Eyes." Show the name card with the word *Church* printed on it. Emphasize to the group that there are many times when we can see the Church doing good things for others. Ask: Have you ever seen the Church give clothing, toys, or food to the poor? What do you see the Church do for the needy at holidays, such as Thanksgiving or Christmas? What do you see young people and grown-ups doing for the sick and lonely? Invite as many children as possible to respond to each question.

◆ **Sharing Together.**   Invite the children to tell what they see the people on pages 132 and 133 doing. Point out the children putting the food into the carton. There is the young girl giving her pretty dress for someone who may not have one. Look at the person carefully folding the donated clothing so that another family can be warm this winter. After they describe what they see, ask for responses to the four questions on page 133.

Inquire where the children think the Love Truck is going. Maybe it will travel only a short distance to people who need our help right here where we live. Or maybe it will travel a long distance, giving our message of love and care to people in another part of the city or in a faraway place.

• You may want to mention organizations or committees in your parish that do special acts of helping. Some people may visit a local hospital or nursing home to cheer up the sick and lonely. Others may bring food and love to shut-ins or campaign for driving safely. Emphasize those parish groups that travel out into your community to show that they know and love Jesus.

◆ **Acting Justly.**   Tell the children we are going to have our own Love Truck collection. We are going to be the Church giving to others. Ask who can bring a toy or book or something they would be willing to give to another child. Have the children bring their items to the next session. Distribute drawing paper and invite the children to add the Love Truck to your parish collage. They might have several Love Trucks filled with clothing and food going to faraway places. Ask what they would put in the Love Truck for others in need.

◆ **Praying Together.**   Gather the children for prayer. Invite them to repeat this prayer after you: "Dear God, we thank you for all the people we see who are the Church. Help us all to love and help one another. Amen."

Think of some things your parish does that help children see what the Church is.

Why are your own actions telling the children about the meaning of Church? Do they see the Church when they see you?

*The Church helps us
to learn, to pray, to grow,
to be fully alive.*

*How is the Church helping
you to learn, pray, grow,
and be fully alive?*

Day 4

◆ **Gathering Together.** Help the children to see the Church by giving them the opportunity to meet some people in our parish Church. Invite your pastor, a lector, or your parish council president to tell the children what they do as a member of the Church. Other guests might include a youth group representative, altar society member, priest, sister, deacon, senior citizen, parish council member, religion program coordinator, or the principal of your parish school.

Before the session, explain to your guests that you and the children have been seeing what the members of the Church do to show God's love in the world. Ask each person to prepare a three-minute talk on his or her role of service in the Church. Be sure the person shares feelings about the importance of this service to the community and the reasons for being involved.

Ask each guest to bring in items that could help the children see what comprises their various duties. A priest might bring in holy oils or a Bible. Your parish council president might have a gavel and minutes from a meeting.

◆ **Sharing Together.** Pages 134 and 135 offer the opportunity for the children to identify some members of the parish. Encourage them to look at the photos to tell who they see. Ask how these people are serving others in the Church in special ways. Help the children to see the ways the Church offers help to learn, to pray, and to care. Go around the group, helping everyone to carefully print, one at a time, your name and the names of the pastor, a lector, and the parish council president in your parish. You may want to print the names on the chalkboard and have the children copy them.

• Sing the first two verses of the Theme Song, "Our Eyes."

◆ **Acting Justly.** Allow time for the guests to talk with the children about the parish. Let some children share what they have learned about how the guests serve others. Ask the children to identify ways the Church has helped them. For example: Parents love and care for their children. Friends cheer up a sad or lonely friend. People visit a sick child. People help when a child is in need. People offer prayers for one another.

• Collect the toys, books, and other things the children brought for children who are in need. Pack them together and tell the children whom you will give them to.

◆ **Praying Together.** Invite your guest or guests to share in the closing prayer service on page 136. Follow the annotations in the guide.

WE SEE OUR PARISH AT MASS

We Pray

Journeying in Faith

The Second Vatican Council, in its *Constitution on the Sacred Liturgy,* called for full, conscious, and active participation of all the faithful in liturgical celebration. It stated that such participation "is demanded by the very nature of the liturgy." It is demanded because liturgy is an action of the entire assembled community.

It is not unusual to hear someone say that the priest is celebrating the Mass. Such a statement manifests a lack of understanding of the nature of liturgy. Liturgy is the action of the community. All members of the assembly are celebrants. The priest is the one who presides at the community's celebration. He serves the community by leading it in prayer. He is called the president of the assembly.

The principal celebrant of the Church's liturgy is Christ risen and present with the Church. In the liturgical celebrations, it is Christ who acts as principal priest. Sacraments are acts of Christ in which the Church as the risen body of Christ acts in union with him.

After Christ as principal celebrant, the primary celebrant of every liturgy is the assembled community. This is why the Council said that full, conscious, and active participation from the faithful is demanded by the very nature of the liturgy.

The idea that all of the faithful are celebrants may seem novel. We were accustomed in the past to thinking of the Mass, for example, as the priest's prayer. We tended to think of the priest as the one who "says" Mass and the people as those who "hear" Mass. It was the priest's actions on which we focused. The people seemed to be onlookers who shared in the benefits of the priest's actions.

What had been forgotten is that through baptism all the members of the Church share in Christ's priesthood. In the scriptures, priesthood belongs primarily and exclusively to Jesus as Lord. Secondarily, it belongs to the whole Church, to all those who share Christ's life and priestly dignity.

Within this community of the faithful, the ordained priest shares in a special way in Christ's priesthood. The ordained priest is empowered by the Church to serve the local community as leader in its liturgical celebrations.

Is my own participation in the liturgy full, concious, and active?

The primary celebrant of every liturgy is the assembled community. How does your parish assembly actively participate in the liturgy?

The ministry of the ordained priest is a ministry of leadership and service. How do you see your parish priests minister in your community?

The Eucharist as the central action of the Church's liturgy is an act of the entire people gathered together. In this action, no one should be a by-stander or onlooker. In its celebration, many members of the community minister to the whole community, and the entire assembly is actively involved in the liturgical action.

The variety of ministries exercised at each Eucharist express the priestly dignity of all. The whole assembled community worships. It sings, pre-pares itself though the penitential rite, thanks God for the word it has heard, joins in the beginning of the eucharistic prayer, and through the great Amen accepts this prayer as its own.

Members of the community minister as ushers or hosts and hostesses who welcome the community and create an environment of hospitality. Others proclaim the readings, lead the assembly in sung prayer, assist the presider, bring forward the gifts, and serve as special ministers of communion.

How does church make itself visible in its worship?

The ordained priest, chosen by the Church to preside at liturgy, ministers in the name of and for all. The ministry of the ordained priest is a ministry of leadership and service. Called by the Church, the ordained priest leads the assembly as it offers worship to the Father, in the name of Christ, and by the power of the Spirit.

The ordained priest cannot be isolated from the community as it worships. This priest is one with the community, leading it as it expresses its faith in prayer. In liturgy, the entire priestly community joins with Christ, the one true priest, and through Christ, the community's action becomes acceptable to the Father.

WE SEE OUR PARISH AT MASS

We Pray

Journeying in Faith with Children

Aims

- To appreciate all the people at Mass who help us to celebrate

New Words

usher	ministers of hospitality
cantor	choir
procession	Holy Communion

Materials

Day 1: • church building outlines
- crayons
- candle

Day 2: • guest tables
- lectionary

Day 3: • crayons
- candles

Day 4: • candle
- flowers
- cross
- Bible
- drawing paper
- crayons or markers

Theme Song

"Our Eyes" from the cassette *Songs for Living Waters 1* by Stephen Chapin

Day 1

◆ **Gathering Together.** Gather the children in the sharing center and sing two verses of the Theme Song, "Our Eyes." Have the collage from last week posted on a nearby wall or bulletin board. Review the concept of Church as people who serve and care for one another.

◆ **Sharing Together.** Point out that these people come together each week to pray in a building we also call the "church." They come together on Saturday evening or on Sunday to celebrate Mass. Use the collage to help the children remember some of the people who are your parish. Recall with them why we come together on Sundays.

Mention that today we are going to hear a story about our friend, Emily. We will see Emily at Mass. We will look right over her shoulder as she sees all that is happening at Mass.

• Direct the children to turn to page 137 in their books. Introduce the story of Emily being at a special Mass for the children and their families at Saint Mark's Church. Read the story to them dramatically while they look at the pictures of people outside of Saint Mark's Church. Point out that our parish is made up of all kinds and sizes of families. Some are small; others are large. Some people are young; others are older. All are welcome. Invite volunteers to share who they see at Mass by naming people they know.

◆ **Acting Justly.** Distribute to each child an outline of the church building that you have duplicated. These outlines should resemble the basic structure of your church but should be kept simple and be large enough for the children to draw inside the outline. Help them to print the name of your parish across the top of the page. Then invite the children to draw themselves and some other people in the parish who help others within the church outline.

• Teach the last verse of the Theme Song, "Our Eyes."

◆ **Praying Together.** Light a candle and close with this simple prayer. Have the children stand and repeat after you: "Dear Jesus, we thank you for all the people we see at Mass. We thank you for our beautiful church building where we come together to celebrate. We are called the Church. Amen."

The people we see at Mass are the Church.

What is your appreciation of what an usher, or minister of hospitality, contributes to the prayer of the community?

Day 2

◆ **Gathering Together.** Invite guests to come and visit with your children and you today. As the children get settled, introduce your guests. Explain to the children that your guests are people who help your parish to pray. Each one does something special when we come together for Mass each week. The guests will describe what they do, and the children will be invited to ask them questions about their ministry.

◆ **Sharing Together.** First, however, continue Emily's story as it appears on pages 138 and 139. Invite the children to look at the pictures and tell what they see. Explain the following Mass words:

Ushers, or ministers of hospitality, are among those people who welcome us to the church. They prepare the church for worship and see that each of us has a seat. They make sure that we have a songbook to help us pray. Ushers are always alert to see if any of us needs assistance.

The *cantor* leads us in singing.

Mass begins with a *procession.* The children most likely have seen the cross and the lectionary being carried in a procession. There is also a procession when the gifts of bread and wine are brought up to the altar. They have seen the people carrying the gifts of bread and wine.

As you read aloud the text at the bottom of page 138, hold up a *lectionary.* Explain that it contains many wonderful stories and sayings from the Bible. Different stories or passages are read aloud by the lector at Mass. The priest or deacon reads the gospel reading.

• Use the text and questions on page 139 to encourage the children to share their own experiences at Mass. They can tell what they have seen ushers do at Mass. They might name some boys or girls whom they have seen in the entrance procession or help as altar servers. Some children may have family members or friends in the choir.

• Sing the Theme Song, "Our Eyes."

◆ **Acting Justly.** Now is the time for you to divide the children into smaller groups to visit with each of your guests. As the children see how each guest helps the parish to pray, urge the children to take part in whatever way they can the next time they are at Mass.

◆ **Praying Together.** Have your guests join the children in a song of joy and celebration. The guests who are ushers could guide the children to the prayer center and seat them in a semicircle. The altar servers might carry the processional cross and Bible. The lector could read an appropriate passage for all to respond to. The cantor or choir members can lead the entire group in a joyful song of praise.

Day 3

◆ **Gathering Together.**   Invite a parish priest to visit with the children. Briefly review with the children those people of the parish whom they have met. Ask the children what they might like to do when they grow old enough to participate in a Church ministry.

• Now introduce the priest to your group. Explain that he has come to talk with us today and that he will tell us how he helps our parish to pray at Mass each week.

◆ **Sharing Together.**   Before the children visit with your guest, have them turn to page 140, which continues Emily's story. Have your group stand and pray the Our Father along with the priest, Father Gerald, in the story. When telling about Emily seeing the people going forward to receive the Holy Bread and Wine, keep to the story. Today is not meant to be a detailed discussion on Holy Communion. As the story concludes, highlight the children in the procession. Emily saw and heard, and she felt happy to be a member of the parish family of Saint Mark's Church.

• Ask your first-graders to name the priest whom they see at Mass and is now in the room. Supply crayons for them to draw his picture in their books. Invite the priest to go around the group and express delight in all his portraits. Invite the children to share with the priest what they like best about belonging to your parish. This is an open-ended discussion and all are to be welcomed and affirmed.

Now is the time for the guest priest or pastor to tell the children how he helps the people pray at Mass.

◆ **Acting Justly.**   Arrange ahead of time with the priest to involve the children in a discussion of what they like best about belonging to your parish. Then have him help the children consider what they can contribute to the parish's mission of caring for and serving others.

• Note: If it is not possible for a priest from the parish to visit with the children, try to arrange to have his picture available and contribute what he might have said.

◆ **Praying Together.**   Invite the priest to lead the children in procession to the prayer center. Help several children light some candles as the group gathers around the prayer table. Ask the priest to offer a blessing for the children and to pray the Our Father with them. Then have everyone share the handshake of peace. The priest may then lead the entire group in singing a closing hymn.

Allow the children time to talk about what they see at Mass.

Of all the things you see happening in your parish, for which are you most grateful?

Day 4

◆ **Gathering Together.** Recall with the children all the people and their ministries they have seen during the week. Explain that today we will hold our own celebration. This will express the joy and love we feel because we belong to our parish and to the Church.

◆ **Sharing Together.** Now explain that we will divide up into groups to help prepare and plan for our celebration of what we have learned about this past week.

Group 1: These children will be responsible for setting up the prayer center. They will arrange the chairs around the prayer table and make sure a candle is placed on the prayer table. You might bring in some flowers to decorate the table. These children will serve as ushers as well.

Group 2: These children will act as members of a procession. One child will carry a cross, another the Bible. The rest of the group will draw pictures of some of the people whom they have met this week and how these people help us to pray. These drawings will be carried by several children in the procession.

Group 3: The children in this group will take turns telling about some wonderful things we have learned during this past week. This should, of course, be kept simple so the children can say their passages at the celebration.

Use pages 143 and 144 to review the entire chapter. These are purposely kept simple to afford a brief, yet meaningful method of recalling the major themes of the last four sessions. Such a review will make the celebration more meaningful.

◆ **Acting Justly.** Ask the children how they, as members of the parish, can serve the parish. Seek specific responses. Help a child to light the candle.

◆ **Praying Together.** The prayer service on page 142 will prove to be a fitting way to conclude your celebration of all the wonderful people in our parish family.

6.
Life Is Good

Looking Ahead

Life is a wonderful gift! In this chapter we will discover who gave us life. Do you think that Jesus loved life? Did He work and play and have fun as we do? We will learn how to praise and thank God for life.

Chapter Aims

OUR LIVES

To become aware of and appreciate what it means to be alive

GOD'S WORD

To appreciate that God gave us people and all of life for our happiness; to realize our responsibility to care for all creation

THE CHURCH

To learn to follow the words of Jesus on how to be happy; to decide how we will praise God through loving acts of kindness to others

WE PRAY

To learn morning and evening prayers of praise and thanks to God

---

**Chapter Six
Theme Song**

"Life Is Good" from the cassette *Songs for Living Waters 1* by Stephen Chapin

---

Using the Chapter Title Page

Invite the children to look at the picture on page 145, the Title Page for Chapter Six. Ask them to suggest why the children in the picture might be dancing and laughing. Help the children to see that we are able to respond happily to many different things in life because we are alive.

After reading the chapter title, preview the chapter by reading the "Looking Ahead" box to the children.

Chapter Plan Ahead

Make arrangements for the following items well in advance of the session in which they are used.

- You will need to prepare five gift wrapped boxes and five cardboard circles. Each box should have a lid that can be easily removed. (Part 1)

- Prepare a banner with the words *Thank you, Lord, for giving us life.* Around the words, place pictures of animals, plants, people, and anything that speaks of life. (Part 2)

- You will need to make "smiley face" badges for each of the children. (Part 3)

- Order and preview the suggested audiovisual material. (Part 1)

Audiovisual References

God's Fine Gifts, VHS, Franciscan Communications, 1229 South Santee St., Los Angeles, CA 90015–2566 (Part 1)

Music for the Prayer Services

"For the Beauty of the Earth" from the *Hymnal for Catholic Students,* #120.

WE ARE ALIVE

Our Lives

Life is the excitement of success and the tears of disappointment. Do you agree? Disagree?

What do you like most about being alive?

Journeying in Faith

We take life for granted. The philosopher may question the meaning of life, the poet may sing about its joys and sorrows, but the majority of us simply accept it as a "given."

The expectant mother thinks about it when she feels new life inside her. Middle-aged men and women may reflect on life when they see it threatened by a terminal illness. The elderly sometimes feel life ebbing away like the sun sinking slowly on the distant horizon. Most of the time, however, we simply live without thinking about what it means to be alive. What does it mean to be alive anyway?

One can find volumes written about "the right to life," and "the quality of life," but little about life itself. These phrases speak important truths, but they tell only a small part of the story. They seem to identify life with existence.

Life, however, is more than merely *being;* it is also *doing.* Life is living: growing and knowing, earning a livelihood, and loving people. Life is playful and whimsical; it is laughter, singing, and dancing. Life is solemn and serious; it is struggle for survival, involving pain and heartache. Life is the excitement of success and the tears of disappointment. Life is discovery, the thrill of new ideas, the joy of new friends, the fascination of new places.

Life is the rapture of love. It is the pleasure of a good meal, the stimulation of a cold shower, the gratification of a warm bath, delight in music, joy in beauty. Life is the art of celebrating: birthdays, weddings, graduations, achievements. Life is sorrowful remembering: leaving home, divorce, mindless tragedies, funerals. What part of this description of life hit home the most as you were reading? Why do you think this was so?

It is obvious that the measure of life exceeds the capacity of stethoscopes, x-ray machines, and brain-scanners. A medical chart is not a biography, the story of one's life. "Life signs" (breathing, heartbeat, and pulse rate) tell little about life itself. The medical profession and research scientists are among the first to confess that life is a mystery.

Although science has uncovered much about the make-up of living cells and the process of reproduction in plants, animals, and humans, life still remains very much a mystery. How does one account for the fact that all life—vegetable, animal, and human—has a certain uniform structure? Another factor that adds to the mystery of life is that, as far as we know now, life is unique to planet earth.

As human beings we can reflect on who we are and where in the future we are going. We can take a creative part in shaping our lives. Is this true in your life?

If human life is to flourish, human beings must protect and foster life in all its forms. How can you help?

There is a hierarchy, a kind of pecking order, of life forms. We speak of lower forms and higher forms of life with human life at the summit. Unlike other living organisms, we can reflect on who we are and where in the future we are going.

Human life is, thus, in many ways a paradox. In the sweep of time, it is less than two million years old, a mere toddler when compared to the mammals buried beneath the debris left behind by the great glaciers. Despite their late appearance, humans are the most complex creatures on Earth today. Like all living organisms, human life depends on environment for survival and well-being.

Unlike other creatures, however, humans create and modify their surroundings to fit their needs. Dependent on nature, we struggle to be independent, to be free from the absolute constraints of environment. We humans, the product of life forces, now struggle to control the very structures that give us life. We are creatures struggling to take an ever more creative part in shaping our lives.

The need to safeguard the environment is now a concern of government and many organizations. It was only a few years ago, however, that prophets who were warning us about pollution were regarded as alarmists and opponents of progress. One of these pioneers whom we already have mentioned is Rachel Carson (1904–1964). She was one of the first to raise her pen in protest. Rachel Carson worked for the U.S. Bureau of Fisheries. In 1951, she wrote a book that became a best seller, *The Sea Around Us*. It presented a beautiful description of the part that the oceans play in begetting and sustaining life. Later, she did another book, *The Silent Spring* (1962), which warned that the irresponsible use of certain pesticides and chemicals was upsetting the delicate balance of nature. The United States Bishops recently wrote a statement, *Renewing the Earth,* which urged all of us to care for all of God's creation, especially the life and dignity of human persons.

PART ONE
WE ARE ALIVE

Journeying in Faith with Children

Our Lives

Aims

- To affirm how good it is to be alive
- To appreciate all we can do, physically and mentally, because we are alive
- To take delight in growing and being alive
- To recognize growing as a sign of life

New Word

life

Materials

Day 1: • cutouts of cake
Day 2: • small statue
        • five cards
        • five paper circles for each child, string
        • crayons or markers
Day 3: • picture or model of an airplane
        • plant
Day 4: • stuffed animal
        • construction paper outlines of boys and girls
        • crayons

Theme Song

"Life Is Good" from the cassette *Songs for Living Waters 1* by Stephen Chapin

Day 1:

◆ **Gathering Together.** Give each child a posterboard cutout of a birthday cake. The cake should have "Happy Birthday _____" written on it. Allow enough room for the child to write his or her name. Talk with the children about birthday parties. Ask what are the "highlight" moments of a party. If any child has celebrated a birthday recently, allow her or him to share the experience with the class. Then have the children write their names on their "cakes" and decorate them. Sing the "Happy Birthday" song together.

◆ **Sharing Together.** Have the children place their decorated posterboard "cakes" on their desks in front of them while you read the birthday party story on page 147 in their book. Tell the story dramatically. Ask the question "What do you think Gran meant?" Pause and allow the children to suggest answers.

• Divide the chalkboard into two columns and print *Alive* at the top of one column and *Not Alive* at the top of the other. Ask the children to look around the room to see if they can find something that is not alive. Some examples might be a pencil, book, desk, window, a piece of chalk, and so on. Follow the same procedure with the other column, but tell the children they might add things that they can find outside, around the school, or on the playground.

◆ **Acting Justly.** Talk again with the children about the wonder of being alive. Explain that besides remembering and celebrating the gift of life on our birthdays, we can show that we appreciate the gift of life by taking good care of it. We take care of life when we eat the right kind of food, exercise, get plenty of rest, and take only medicine that our doctor and parents give to us. We take care of life when we refuse to hurt others.

◆ **Praying Together.** Gather the children in the prayer center. Have them place their posterboard "cakes" on a table in the middle of the group. Tell them they will now have a prayer celebration to thank God for the wonderful gift of life. Sing the following lyrics together to the tune of "Happy Birthday."

> We thank you, dear God, we thank you for life.
> We thank you, dear God, we thank you for life.

What do you consider the greatest gift you have ever received?

What is the greatest gift you have given to another person?

Day 2

◆ **Gathering Together.** Place a statue on the desk in the front of the room where each child can see it. Ask the group to look closely at the statue for a few minutes so that they can answer some questions about it.

Ask the children whether the statue can see and hear, touch and feel, taste and smell, walk and run, jump and play, and so on. When finished, talk about why the statue could not do any of these things. Have the children pretend they are statues and stand very still for a few minutes. When finished, ask whether they would like to have to stand that way always! Talk about the wonderful things we can do because we are alive.

◆ **Sharing Together.** On your desk have five cards, each of which has a simple drawing of a sensing part of the body: eyes, ears, hands, mouth, or nose. Invite volunteers to come and pick out a card and tell the class what wonderful things we can do with that gift. Call on others to add to their suggestions. After each child's response, ask why it is that we can do these things. Invite the children to respond with "We are alive!" Adapt this if children with disabilities are present.

• Have the children turn to pages 148 and 149 in their books. Read the things that they can do because they are alive. Invite the children to use gestures, such as touching their eyes, taking a few steps, hopping, and so on, as you read along. Then invite them to tell a story about what is happening in each part of the illustration.

• Give each child five paper circles with a hole punched in the top of each. Each set of five circles has one of the following written on each paper circle: "Life is good." "I can hear." "I can touch and move." "I can taste and smell." "I can see." Ask the children to draw a picture on the other side of each circle, showing how they can do what is written on the circle. Tie the circles together with string to make mobiles and hang these around the room.

• Teach the first verse of the Theme Song, "Life Is Good."

◆ **Acting Justly.** Talk with the children about how grateful we should be for these wonderful gifts of life. Ask them for suggestions about how we can use these gifts. Brainstorm as a group some ways to act. Ask the children to choose one of these suggestions to work on during this week.

◆ **Praying Together.** Gather in the prayer center and ask the children to join hands. Join with the children and together walk slowly around in a circle singing to the tune of "Happy Birthday" the lyrics they learned on the previous day.

Day 3

◆ **Gathering Together.** Begin by gathering the children in the sharing center. Sing the first verse of the Theme Song, "Life Is Good." Show the children a picture or model of an airplane. Tell them that today they will discover more of the wonderful powers they have because they are alive. The picture or model will help them understand these powers.

◆ **Sharing Together.** Ask the children whether any of them have ever flown in an airplane. Let them share any experiences they have had. Explain that years ago, there were no airplanes. Tell them the story of the Wright brothers.

> There were two brothers named Orville and Wilbur Wright who were always asking questions. When Orville and Wilbur watched the birds flying in the air, they asked, "Why can birds fly? Can we fly?" They began to picture in their minds something that no one had ever seen before, a machine that could fly! They were using the gift of their imagination.
>
> One day after thinking, wondering, imagining, they made a flying machine. Everyone was so excited as they watched the brothers take off in their flying machine. It was the first time anyone had ever been able to fly!

• Have the children open their books to page 150 and read it together. Talk with them about some of the wonderful things they can do. Help them do the activity on the page.

Show the children a plant. Explain how it began as a little seed and how it slowly grew until it became a beautiful plant. Ask the children whether they can grow, too, and have them tell why. Then invite them to share stories about how they have outgrown clothes, how they are now able to tie their own shoes, zip their own jackets, and so on. Help them discover they have learned these things as they have grown. Help them to get excited about the fact that they are able to grow. Growing is a part of living.

◆ **Acting Justly.** Ask the children to imagine what they could do to help others when they themselves grow up. Then have them tell what can they do to help others today.

Ask them to read page 151 with you. Then direct them to do the activity. Point out that they are now able to do things for others because they have grown.

◆ **Praying Together.** Review with the children the gifts God has given us. Lead the children in the following prayer: "We thank you, God, for giving us the power to use all the gifts you have given us. Amen."

God gave us the gift of life. Think about how fragile this gift is.

How can we protect the gift of life? How can we nurture it?

We have the gift of life so that we can work together as a happy family. Do you see this being lived out?

Thank you, God, for the gift of life.

Day 4

◆ **Gathering Together.** Begin by singing the first verse of the Theme Song, "Life Is Good."

Tape large letters spelling the word *life* in incorrect order to the chalkboard. Ask the children to look at the letters to see if they can find a word that tells what they have been learning about this week. Call on a child to come and place the letters in order.

◆ **Sharing Together.** Show the children a stuffed animal. Give the animal a name. Have them admire it and touch it. Point to the word *life* on the chalkboard. Then ask: "Does this stuffed animal have life?" "How do you know?" Ask whether any of the children have a live pet at home. Have those who do tell the class a little about their pet. Then ask, "What can your pet do that this stuffed animal cannot do?" Have all the children suggest as many things as possible that pets can do. Talk with them about why the live animal can do so much more.

◆ **Acting Justly.** Pass out one construction paper outline of a boy or girl to each child. Talk with the children about the difference between the life they have as persons and the life of their pets. Recall with the children the powers they have received with life: the power to think, wonder, remember, and imagine. Lead them to a sense of wonder and gratitude to God for all the wonderful gifts of life they have received. Pass out crayons and have each child write in the paper outline they have received some of the things they can do because they are alive. Have them print their names as well. Have them talk about how the things they do can help others.

◆ **Praying Together.** Invite the children to gather in the prayer center. Have them bring their outlines with them and stand in a semicircle around a table. Ask them to think about the wonderful gifts of life that they have just been talking about. Tell them to think of one that they would especially like to thank God for.

Then begin with the Sign of the Cross. Continue with the rest of the prayer as suggested on page 152. See the suggested activities in the annotated guide.

GOD GIVES US LIFE

God's Word

When we nurture life, we collaborate in God's creative art. In what ways do you nurture life?

✍

Do you agree that wisdom is the key to life? Why or why not?

✍

Journeying in Faith

The phrase, "the origin of life," means different things to different people. For the ancient Greek, it evoked the image of the goddess of fertility, Aphrodite, emerging fully developed from the foam of the sea. For the modern scientist, it conjures up one of those "genetic moments" when inanimate matter crossed the threshold to become a living organism. For the student of the Bible, it brings to mind the accounts in Genesis.

First God made heaven and earth. Then God separated the dry land from the waters. On the third day God created life.

In the last stages of creation, God created higher forms of life, the cattle, reptiles, and the like. Finally, on the sixth day, as a fitting climax to the work of creation, God called forth human life. The Bible carefully distinguishes it from other forms of life. Of all the creatures, only humans are said to be made in God's image and likeness.

A basic premise of ecology is that "all living things, without exception, depend on other living things for their survival and development." Modern scientists understand this principle in terms of matter and physical relationships. Biblical authors accept the same principle, but they apply it to all of reality, the spiritual as well as the material. Ultimately all life comes from and is sustained by the living God. In fact, it is because God is seen as the source and creator of all life that "the living God" is one of God's most esteemed titles. Thus, when human beings bring forth and nurture life, we collaborate in God's creative act.

Life is the first grace we receive. Life is total gift. We do nothing to earn it or even to dispose ourselves for it. God took the initiative. Because it comes from God, all life and especially human life is sacred.

God not only gives us life, but also provides the elements necessary to sustain life. The powerful creation hymn that parallels the Genesis account and that we read as Psalm 104, praises the Lord for the sun and moon, for the rain and grass and trees, for cattle, for birds, and for the immeasurable sea. It praises God for "wine to gladden people's hearts and oil to make their faces shine and bread to sustain their strength."

According to the biblical teaching, wisdom is the key to life, the art of living. Wisdom's good life is a long life of peace, family harmony, a good name, the love of friends, and moderate wealth.

Do you agree that the option we have is to choose life and good or death and evil? What examples come to mind from your experiences?

The ultimate measure of wisdom is God's law: to follow God's law is to have life. The link between life and God's law is basic to God's relationship to people. Life is grace and opportunity. As long as one has life, the possibility of change, of growth, of improvement remains. It is the occasion for becoming what we are called to be. Life means choosing. It is saying "yes," affirming ourselves and affirming our relationship to God and neighbor. Think for a moment about how you will say "yes" to life today.

The *Didache,* a Christian writing almost as old as the New Testament, is known also as "The Teaching of the Twelve Apostles." It begins by saying that there are two ways, one of life and one of death. The *Didache* describes the way of life as loving God who made you, and loving your neighbor as yourself. It suggests that whatever you would not like done to you, do not do to another. The way of life is loving one's enemy, being generous to those in need, and fleeing wickedness.

On the other hand, the *Didache* describes the way of death as evil and full of cursings, murders, adulteries, evil desires, fornications, thefts, and idolatries. The way of death includes magical practices, sorceries, robberies, false witnessings, hypocrisies, and double-mindedness. The way of death is full of guile, pride, malice, arrogance, covetousness, filthy talk, envy, insolence, haughtiness, and lack of fear of God.

How will you choose life today?

The *Didache* is saying in modern language: these vices are suicidal. They kill the possibility of growth and slowly choke off life. This is the option that the Lord God offers, the choice of life and good, or death and evil. Choose life!

PART TWO
GOD GIVES US LIFE

God's Word

Aims

- To learn that life is a gift from God
- To appreciate that people are the greatest part of God's creation
- To appreciate that God gave us life and continues to give us life
- To be aware of our responsibilities to care for others and for God's creation

New Word

creation

Materials

Day 1: • pictures of children
- construction paper circles
- string
- crayons
- two sticks attached in the form of a cross

Day 2: • Bible
- quiet background music

Day 3: • none

Day 4: • gift boxes cut out of drawing paper
- pencils
- construction paper

Theme Song

"Life Is Good" from the cassette *Songs for Living Waters 1* by Stephen Chapin

Journeying in Faith with Children

Day 1

◆ **Gathering Together.** Begin by gathering the children and singing the first verse of the Theme Song, "Life Is Good." Show pictures of children engaged in such various activities as playing, running, laughing, and so on. Ask the children what they see happening in each picture and how they think the children in the pictures feel. Explain that in today's lesson they will learn about all the wonderful things that we and these children can do because we have the gift of life.

◆ **Sharing Together.** Have the children open their books to page 153 and respond to the first statement. List on the chalkboard the things they say they can do because they are alive. Point to one response at a time and ask one or two of the children to dramatize the actions. Lead them to see that all of these things are possible for them to do because God has given them this wonderful gift of life.

Continue reading page 153. Enjoy and discuss each of the illustrated creatures. Invite the children to come up one at a time and tell the group one thing that they can do that an animal cannot do.

• Make a "life-mobile." Pass out a circle cut from construction paper to each child. Then ask the children to draw a picture of themselves doing one of the favorite things they can do because they are alive. Tie a string to each circle and attach the strings to two sticks tied together in the form of a cross.

◆ **Acting Justly.** Thank God for the gift of life. Before attaching their drawings to the sticks to make a "life-mobile," invite the children to share their drawings of themselves. Remind them that when they are doing any of these happy activities, they are using the gift of life that God has given to them. Ask them to name one way they can help something or someone who is alive.

◆ **Praying Together.** Gather in the prayer center. Ask the children to close their eyes and to be very still for a few moments. Invite them to think about the words you speak. Pray the following phrases slowly and quietly, and have the children respond "Alleluia" after each one:

> I am alive!
> God has given me the wonderful gift of life!

Conclude by singing the first verse of the Theme Song, "Life Is Good."

Thank you, Lord, for giving us life. Help us nurture and enrich your gift.

We see God's love in all the things we have been given that help us enjoy life.

Day 2

◆ **Gathering Together.**   Begin by singing the first verse of the Theme Song, "Life Is Good." Invite the children to suggest actions to go with the words of the song. Remind the children that they have been learning about the wonderful gift of life God has given them.

◆ **Sharing Together.**   Show them a Bible. Explain that the Bible tells us a wonderful secret about the people God made. Have the children open their books to page 154 to see whether they can find the words from the Bible. Read the scriptural quote to them. On the chalkboard, print *God created people to be like God.*

• Read the next two lines on page 154. Talk about how excited manufacturers of dolls are when they can make dolls that do such things as talking, crying, walking, and so on. If you have a doll that does one of these things, you might bring it in and show it to the children. Talk with them about the difference between a doll and a real person. The doll cannot do these things by itself; the doll cannot love or help others.

Continue reading the rest of page 154. List on the chalkboard some things people can do that make them like God: love, help one another, and enjoy one another.

• Teach the second verse of the Theme Song, "Life Is Good."

• Have the children look carefully at the picture on pages 154 and 155. Talk about what the children in the picture are doing. Ask them if they can do these things and have them tell why. Point out that the children in the picture are making something new. Help them to see that when we make something new we are like God, who made everything in this beautiful world for us.

◆ **Acting Justly.**   Read page 155 and ask the children to listen carefully for four ways in which we can share the gift of life. When finished, write numbers from 1 through 4 on the chalkboard and ask the children to read the four ways one at a time from the book. List them on the chalkboard. Have the children examine the picture in their book and tell if they think the children in the picture are doing any of these four things. Encourage the children to do something to share life.

◆ **Praying Together.**   Play some quiet background music. Have the children close their eyes and try to be very still inside themselves as they listen to this prayer: "God, how wonderful you are to give us the wonderful gift of life! Thank you, God, for giving us this gift of life to enjoy. Teach us to share it by helping others to know you better and to love you more."

Have all the children respond, "Amen."

Day 3

◆ **Gathering Together.**   Begin by singing the first and second verses of the Theme Song, "Life Is Good." Invite the children to suggest actions to go with the words.

Elicit from the children some of the things they have learned about the world. There are the lands and the oceans, the different countries, the things that grow in different parts of the world, and so on. Talk about how beautiful the world that God gave us is. It was God's special gift of love.

◆ **Sharing Together.**   Have the children open their books to pages 156 and 157. Read the verse from Genesis and explain to the children that this is from the very first part of the Bible. Help them discover that God tells us here that God made people very special. Read "Let people be above" and let the children complete the sentence, reading it from their books.

Ask them what the next sentence tells us about what the children in the pictures are doing. Have them read the sentence together. Then ask the two questions at the bottom of page 156. Explain how caring for the world is not just something that God wants adults to do. Children, too, have a part in helping to keep our world beautiful and healthy.

◆ **Acting Justly.**   Then talk about how some children who receive gifts do not take very good care of them. Ask them how they think most people take care of this great world God has given us. Lead them to see that God wants us to be loving, not only with people, but with all things in the world. This is because God gave us these things to make our lives better.

Read page 157 and have them do the activity at the bottom of the page. Ask individuals to tell what is happening in each of the pictures. Have them tell which one they checked and explain why.

◆ **Praying Together.**   Gather in the prayer center. Pray the following litany with the children:

Catechist: You gave us life.
           We thank you, God.

Children: We thank you, God!

Catechist: You made us to be like you.

Children: We thank you, God!

Catechist: You have given us a beautiful world to care for
           and to enjoy.
           We thank you, God.

Children: We thank you, God!
All: Amen.

God wants all children and adults to be caring and loving, not only with all people, but with all things in creation. How can you do this?

What happens when people do not care for God's creation? Does this make a difference where you live?

How do you show how grateful you are for God's creation?

Day 4

◆ **Gathering Together.** Begin by singing the first two verses of the Theme Song, "Life Is Good." Recall with the children what they have learned about life. Talk about how God created people to be like God. Emphasize that God gives us the gift of life. Invite the chilidren to suggest ways that people can love and help one another and all of creation.

◆ **Sharing Together.** Give each child a sheet of drawing paper cut in the shape of a gift box with a tag marked "From God." Tell them to print at the top the name of a gift from God they have been learning about. Then talk with them about the important points they have learned about the gift of life. Encourage the children to look back at all the pictures in the chapter they have been covering this past week. Help them recall that people are special, that God wants us to share our gift of life, and that God wants us to care for our beautiful world.

◆ **Acting Justly.** Choose to care for our world. Give each child a strip of construction paper. On each strip have these words written: "I will care for my world by _____ ." Invite the children to think of one thing they can do to care for our world. Help them to complete the sentence by writing their choice on the strip of paper. Let them share what they have written if they would like to do so. Ask them to bring their strips to the prayer center with them.

◆ **Praying Together.** Gather in the prayer center. Following the annotations, lead the children in the prayer on page 158. After the question, "What can we do this week to take care of our earth?" have each child come forward to give you her or his strip. Staple all the strips of construction paper together to make a "Caring Circle Chain" and place this on the prayer table as a reminder to the children of how they will care for our world. Then finish the last part of the prayer and have the children respond, "Amen."

You may wish to teach the hymn "For the Beauty of the Earth" from the *Hymnal for Catholic Students,* #120.

JESUS LOVED LIFE

The Church

"I am the way, the truth, and the life; no one goes to the Father except by me." How does this saying of Jesus' affect your life?
🖎

Do you find it difficult to imagine Jesus laughing, crying, and fully experiencing life as He lived it? Why or why not?
🖎

Journeying in Faith

There is a striking parallel between the opening words of Genesis and those of St. John's gospel: "In the beginning. . . ." The similarity is not a matter of chance. The author of John's gospel wanted to situate the story of Jesus in the broad sweep of the creation story.

All the gospel writers emphasize Jesus' regard for life. In Matthew, we find him saying that life is more than food. In Mark, saving a life is more important than Sabbath observance, because God is not God of the dead but of the living. In Luke, the young man asks what he must do to win eternal life.

But it is in the gospel according to John that the theme of life is most emphasized. He repeats Jesus' saying, "I am the way, the truth, and the life; no one goes to the Father except by me" (John 14:6).

The life that Jesus speaks of is eternal, that is, unending life that even death cannot destroy. In John's gospel, life says it all. It includes those mysteries that Matthew, Mark, and Luke refer to with different words, such as Kingdom of God, salvation, healing, and forgiveness.

The gift of life is the purpose of Jesus' mission: "I have come in order that you might have life—life in all its fullness" (John 10:10). It is a call for humans to share in the life of God. Thus it is in Jesus that divine life and human life converge. We call it the Incarnation, the enfleshing of the divine in a human being.

Jesus was true God and true man. "Jesus Christ, dwelt among us and worked with his hands, thought with a human mind, acted with a human will, loved with a human heart. This man is truly the Word and the Son of God."

Think about all the feelings and experiences you have had throughout your life as a human being. Reflect on how Jesus was not immune from all those same feelings and experiences in the life he lived. He laughed and cried just as we do in trying to keep up with all that life sends our way.

Jesus reveals that God is our Father, and he also reveals what it means to be human. He makes known to us that our supreme calling is to be one with God. Jesus suffered not only for us but with us. He experienced fear and worry as well as physical pain. He "provided us with an example for our imitation. He blazed a trail, and if we follow it, life and death are made holy and take on a new meaning."

*Why do you think
God make you?*

The first question in the old catechisms asked: "Why did God make you?" The question could be rephrased to ask: "What is the meaning of life?" The eminent Cardinal Archbishop of Louvain, Belgium, Leon Joseph Suenens, while traveling on a lecture tour throughout the United States several years ago, used to ask his audience this same question: "Why did God make you?"

Cardinal Suenens would suggest that God made us to know God and to make God known. God made us to serve God and to lead others to serve God. This is the meaning of life as Jesus, the Way, the Truth, and the Life lived it out for us. Knowing, loving, and serving God, together, brings fullness of life in this world and in the world to come.

Dear Catechist,

If you set up the environment as suggested, you may find that moving from space to space is distracting. But as you and the children become more familiar with your "spaces," you will realize how helpful it is to have these places. The sharing center will become not only a place but a time for discovery and listening together.

Of all the factors that influence environment, nothing compares with the environment created by "people relationships." In a catechetical environment, the catechist is the model for all the relationships that develop. Several suggestions can help you create a personal environment that calls out the best in the children.

* Be a good listener. Lead children in discussion, but do not dominate. Listen attentively, even when what the children are saying seems to be a digression. When necessary, gently lead them back to the topic being considered.

* Speak softly. Loudness generates more loudness. Because of the noise level in which we live, a soft voice attracts attention.

* Be respectful to each child. Call each one by name, and compliment the children whenever possible. We all respond positively to compliments and affirmations.

* Don't be afraid to laugh with the children.

* Set guidelines for behavior with the children so that they know what is expected of them. Start and end each session right on time. That's a guideline for your own behavior.

JESUS LOVED LIFE

Journeying in Faith with Children

The Church

Aims

- To affirm the abilities gained this year
- To rejoice in the truth that Jesus is truly human like us
- To appreciate that Jesus tells us how to be happy
- To consider ways to be happy and to share our happiness with others

New Words

alive
grateful

Materials

Day 1: • drawing paper
- crayons

Day 2: • none

Day 3: • envelope containing the letters *H,A,P,P,Y* on five separate squares
- pencils or crayons

Day 4: • paper for life-size outlines
- crayons
- scissors
- candle for prayer
- water for prayer

Theme Song

"Life Is Good" from the cassette *Songs for Living Waters 1* by Stephen Chapin

Day 1

◆ **Gathering Together.** Begin by singing the first two verses of the Theme Song, "Life Is Good." Then focus on topics discussed all year. Look at opening pages of each chapter and share what you and the children have learned. Ask the children to think about one thing that they have learned to do this year that they can tell the whole group. When all are ready, have them share what they have learned.

◆ **Sharing Together.** Invite the children to open their books to page 159. Ask them to find the sentence that tells why we can learn and do all the things that they have mentioned in the discussion. Have them point to the sentence "We are alive!" Read it aloud together. Continue by reading the next two sentences.

• Discuss the pictures. Have the children examine the illustration on page 159. Then question them about each person pictured. Ask such questions as "Why do you think this person looks so happy? Do you think the person is glad to be alive?"

Tell the children that they are going to use a wonderful power called imagination that God has given us. Explain that with this wonderful power we can make pictures in our minds. Invite all the children to close their eyes. Ask them to picture in their minds their favorite thing to do at home. Then give each child a sheet of drawing paper and ask each one to draw a picture of his or her favorite thing. Let each one share his or her picture with the group.

◆ **Acting Justly.** Talk with the children about the fact that each of us enjoys doing different things and that even though we all share the gift of life in common, God has given everyone different gifts. One way we can show God we are grateful for the gift of life is to let others know we are happy that they have their gifts. For example, we can say, "You are a good reader" or "You are a good friend." Encourage the children to do this.

◆ **Praying Together.** Gather in the prayer center. Ask the children to bring their drawings with them. Invite each child to place her or his drawing on the table and say, "Thank you, God, for giving me life so that I can _____ ." Have the child complete the sentence by mentioning what she or he has drawn. Thank God for one of your own favorite things, too.

Thank you, God, for the gift of life. You have made each of us in a wonderful way.

Jesus was like us in many ways. Can you think of some examples of how Jesus was like us?

Day 2

◆ **Gathering Together.** Begin by gathering the children and singing the first two verses of the Theme Song, "Life Is Good." Then explain to the children that they have learned a great deal about life and about how God wants them to live life. Tell them that this week they will be learning about a special person who has shown us how God wants us to live that life. They will be learning about Jesus.

◆ **Sharing Together.** Have the children open their books to pages 160 and 161 and look at the picture. Ask the children to guess the age of Jesus in the picture. Then talk about what Jesus is doing. Ask: "What other things do you think Jesus might have done when he was growing up?"

Lead the children to see that Jesus was like them. Read together page 160 to help them discover what some of those ways were. Recall some of the things that they mentioned earlier that they liked to do. Ask the two questions on page 160 and elicit responses from the whole group. Some of the children may be familiar with the work carpenters do. Encourage them to share their experiences with the group.

Talk with the children about the kinds of work their parents do. See if they can tell from the picture what kind of work Mary and Joseph did. Point out that Mary took care of the house, did the cooking, watched after Jesus, and so on. Talk about what Joseph did as a carpenter. Then read page 161 to them.

◆ **Acting Justly.** Tell the children that we know that Jesus loved his mother, Mary. The gospels do not tell us much about Jesus and his relationship with Joseph. But we know Jesus loved Mary and Joseph. Ask: "How can you show your love for your mother today? How can you show your love for your father?"

◆ **Praying Together.** Gather in the prayer center. Invite the children to respond "Thank you, God, for sending Jesus to us" to each sentence that you say. Then say the following quietly and slowly, pausing for their response after each sentence:

> Jesus lived a long time ago.
> Jesus liked to play and have fun.
> Jesus learned to read and write.
> Jesus did everything with love and care.
> Help us to be like Jesus.

Day 3

♦ **Gathering Together.** Consider what happiness is. Write *Jesus wants us to be _____* on the chalkboard. Open an envelope with big letters *H,A,P,P,Y,* which have been written on five separate squares. Read the incomplete sentence on the chalkboard and tell the children that the letters to spell the missing word are in the envelope. Then call on someone to arrange the letters. Tape them to the chalkboard to complete the sentence.

Ask what the completed sentence tells us about Jesus. Point out that if a person wants you to be happy, it means she or he loves you very much. Ask the children to name people who want them to be happy, such as parents, grandparents, others at home, teachers, friends, and so on. Tell the children that you, too, want them to be happy.

♦ **Sharing Together.** Read the message of Jesus on page 162. Look at the pictures and have the children tell the ways the people in each picture are showing their love for God. Then have them respond to the final question.

• Teach the third verse of the Theme Song, "Life Is Good."

Ask the children whether they remember the Great Commandment that they studied earlier in the year. If so, have them repeat it. If not, help them recall it (pages 106–107). Remind them that it has two parts: to love God and to love others. Loving others is the second thing Jesus tells us to do if we want to be truly happy.

♦ **Acting Justly.** Explore with the children the questions on page 163. Ask them to think of a precise answer to the question about how they help people to be happy. Elicit responses to this question from each child.

• Then pass out pencils or crayons for them to draw a picture in their books of how they can make their family happy. Help them to choose specific things that they can do. As they are drawing, walk around and comment on their pictures. Suggest that they take their book home and share their pictures with their families.

♦ **Praying Together.** Gather in the prayer center. Tell the children to remember what they have drawn about how they will make their family happy. Have them repeat after you: "Jesus, we thank you for teaching us how to be happy. We want to share our happiness with others. Amen."

Jesus wants us to be happy. Do you believe this?

If a person wants you to be happy, it means that he or she loves you very much. What is your experience of this?

If we want to be happy, Jesus says that we should love God and love others.

Day 4

◆ **Gathering Together.**   Begin by singing the song "If You're Happy." Use verses like: clap your hands, stamp your feet, jump up high, all join hands, blink your eyes, and so on.

◆ **Sharing Together.**   Review with the children what they have learned about life. Emphasize how wonderful life is because we can see, hear, and feel. Talk with them about swimming, jumping rope, and some of the other fun activities they can do because they are alive. Ask for volunteers to pantomime some of these activities.

Invite the children to draw a life-size outline of themselves on a large sheet of paper. Have two children work together to help each other. Cut the shapes out and print *I am alive* on each one. Have the children write within their outlines things they can do because they are alive. Let them take the figures home and share them with their families.

• Sing all the verses of the Theme Song, "Life Is Good." Invite the children to suggest actions to interpret the words and music.

◆ **Acting Justly.**   Tell the children to take time today to notice someone who might look sad or lonely and to think about what they can do to make him or her happy.

◆ **Praying Together.**   Gather the children in a circle. Have a lighted candle on a table in the middle of the circle. Give the children a few moments to become quiet and still inside themselves. Then lead them in the prayer service found on page 164, following the annotations.

You may wish to include the hymn "For the Beauty of the Earth" from the *Hymnal for Catholic Students,* #120.

PART FOUR
PRAISE GOD FOR LIFE

We Pray

Life itself is worth celebrating, and sharing life is part of the celebration.
How do you celebrate life?

Sacramental celebrations are community actions celebrating Christian life. Think of a sacrament you celebrate with your parish. What dimension of life is ritualized in the celebration?

Journeying in Faith

Consciousness of life is a uniquely human phenomenon. Being conscious of its beauty and its sorrow rhythmically interchange. At times, awareness of life's goodness captivates us, and we rejoice. At times, tragedy or suffering come to the fore, and we struggle to understand what life is about. Much of the time the concerns of daily life keep us from reflecting on life's meaning.

But when a special occasion comes along, such as a holiday or an anniversary, we want to acknowledge it. People come together to share the joy or the sorrow with us. We gather for weddings, birthdays, accomplishments, and happy events. In sickness and death, we assemble to share our common pain. Life itself is worth celebrating, and sharing life is part of the celebration. Our celebrations, whatever the event, follow a certain pattern. We celebrate with others. Special events call for celebration at a dinner or banquet. Someone is responsible for planning the event. Another person may preside at the meal. There are places of honor. Masters of ceremony lead in presenting awards. People lead with toasts to the new bride and groom. Music fit for the occasion is chosen. There is a beginning, a climax, and a closing for the party.

All of this is a ritual way of solemnizing an occasion. We do not call it ritual, but that is what it is. We plan the special event according to the nature of the celebration. For different occasions, such as birthdays or wedding dinners, the ritual differs, but the celebration is the same. It is a celebration of life-shared.

The Christian community celebrates its shared life in its sacramental celebrations. Each sacramental celebration is ritualized in a different way, because each celebrates a different dimension of life. Sacramental celebrations are community actions. They are ways in which Christians come together to celebrate Christian life.

Christian life differs from non-Christian life in that the meaning of life is perceived through the eyes of Christian faith. We may see the same realities as non-Christians, but our understanding and response to these realities is colored by our acceptance of Jesus as Lord of Life. In accepting Jesus as Lord, we accept a particular meaning of life, as well as a past, present, and future that are different because of that meaning. Life itself is recognized not only as gift from God, but also as a sharing in the life of the Divine.

In what way does your family ritualize birthdays, holidays, graduations, and anniversaries?

Christian life is Trinitarian. The life of the Trinity is a shared life. The Father, the Son, and the Holy Spirit share the one life of God. Trinitarian life is a community of life. The Three are One in love. The Three share their life with us through Christ who became human so that we might have a human vision of the fullness of life. It is his shared life with one another, and with the Father and the Spirit through Christ, that we celebrate in Christians sacraments. All sacramental celebrations are Trinitarian. All are shared life celebrations.

We celebrate entrance into the shared life of the Christian community in baptism and confirmation. When we have estranged or alienated from community life, we celebrate reunion of life in the sacrament of reconciliation. We celebrate new life together in matrimony. The call to service to the community by building up its life is celebrated in orders. In sickness, we celebrate the unity we share with the sick, a unity which heals broken spirits and sick bodies. Our central and most important celebration is the eucharist, a celebration of thanksgiving for our shared life with one another through Christ.

How do you celebrate your Christian life?

We ritualize each of these celebrations of life in a different way, just as we ritualize birthdays, holidays, graduations, and anniversary celebrations in different ways. At all sacramental celebrations, we gather together, we sing, we listen, we speak, and sometimes we dance in procession. Our primary celebration takes the form of a meal, as do most of life's more important celebrations. Christians gather around the table of the Lord, and with bread and wine, which symbolize all the food and drink of life, we praise the Father through Christ for life. We call upon the Spirit to bless the food and drink we offer through Christ to the Father. The Father in turn responds by offering this holy food and drink to us as the sustenance of life. And so we share the one bread as we eat together, and we share the cup of our salvation as we drink the sacred wine.

Sacraments are celebrations of life, shared life. All the glory and pain of life are brought to these celebrations and shared. In sacramental celebrations, we remember that the source of life is in the Trinity, and that the life we live has been divinized by the gift of life which the Trinity gives. This is the mystery. In the life of Jesus, the apostolic community saw the paschal mystery lived out through the sacraments. We share in this paschal mystery by sharing in the life of the church, which is the life of Christ present now in our midst.

152

PART FOUR
PRAISE GOD FOR LIFE

We Pray

Journeying in Faith with Children

Aims

- To express praise and gratitude to God in prayer and service
- To become familiar with a prayer of praise to God
- To sing and pray and praise happily

New Word

praise

Materials

Day 1: • small cutouts of "gift" boxes
        • large gift
Day 2: • picture of a young boy
Day 3: • pencils or crayons
        • large sheet of poster-board
Day 4: • large roll of paper

Theme Song

"Life Is Good" from the cassette *Songs for Living Waters 1* by Stephen Chapin

Day 1

◆ **Gathering Together.** Begin the session with a "gift" hunt. Have small cutouts of a gift box hidden around the room. On each "box" write a gift from God that we have received: hearing, seeing, feeling, etc. Prepare these as a review of the year's work by thumbing through the children's book. Invite the children to search the room until they find one and then to return to their places. Give them a few minutes to examine the writing on the back of each cutout.

◆ **Sharing Together.** Have the children come to the front of the room, one at a time, to tell everything they remember learning about the gift mentioned on the particular box. Encourage the children to clap after each presentation. When they are finished, show them a large box and ask if they would like to hear the names of some very special gifts you have received from God. Read their names, which you have written on the back of the box, and tell them how grateful you are for each of them and for all the wonderful gifts that each child has been given by God.

• Read page 165 to the children. Have the children note the balloon drawing. Lead them to see that the greatest gift we have received from God is the gift of life. Allow time for the children to draw on the balloons what they like best about being alive. Go around to the children as they are drawing and praise each one's work.

◆ **Acting Justly.** When the children have finished their drawings, ask whether they liked hearing your words of praise. Point out to them that God likes to hear words of praise from us, too. Read the last sentence on the page and together praise God for the gift of life. Suggest that the children say some short words of praise to God often during the day, especially when something happens that gives them joy. Ask them to name things they can do to make people happy.

◆ **Praying Together.** Work together with the children to compose a litany of praise. Begin the litany for them with an example and then have them add to the list. The following are some suggestions:

Catechist: Let our eyes   *Children:* praise the Lord!
Catechist: Let our hands *Children:* praise the Lord!

Move to the prayer center. Invite the children to use gestures as they pray.

153

*Think about all the gifts
we have received from God.
Share your feelings
of gratitude.*

*We give praise and
glory to God.*

Day 2

◆ **Gathering Together.** Begin by singing all the verses to the Theme Song, "Life Is Good." Draw a chalkboard diagram using stick figures or show a picture of a young boy to illustrate the following incident. Have the children imagine the situation as you read it to them.

> Roger gets up in the morning and goes down into the kitchen for breakfast. His mother is there cooking breakfast with his sister, Stella. No one speaks to him as he enters.

> Ask the children how they think this would make Roger feel.

> Now imagine it is evening and time for Roger to go to bed. Before going to his room, Roger goes into the living room where everyone is watching TV. He says, "Good night, everyone," and no one answers. How would Roger feel?

Reflect on how important it is to pay attention to others. Ask the children why Roger would have been hurt. Impress on them the fact that we like people to pay attention to us, by greeting us when they see us in the morning, at night, and any time at all. Our expressions "Good morning" and "Good night" are our way of noticing others and paying attention to them.

Explain that people everywhere in the world have words to greet other people when they see them. If you have any children who speak languages other than English, ask them to say "Good morning" or "Good night" in their language. Point out that when people greet us, it helps us realize that we are important.

◆ **Sharing Together.** Explain that God also wants to be greeted by us in the morning and at night. Have the children look at the pictures on pages 166 and 167 and have them listen to you as you read the story about greeting God to them. Ask the children to join in with you as you read the morning prayer on page 166.

◆ **Acting Justly.** Talk with the children about how they might take special care to notice people during the coming week and to greet them in a friendly and warm way. Have them act out how they might do this at home and at school. Encourage them to make a habit of greeting people with a smile.

◆ **Praying Together.** Have the children gather around the prayer table in a circle. Ask them to think quietly about how wonderful and good God is. Then lead them in the following adaptation of Psalm 47:

> All you peoples, clap your hands.
> Shout to God with gladness!
> Sing praise to God, sing praise!
> Sing praise to our King, sing praise!

End the prayer by singing "Alleluia!"

Day 3

◆ **Gathering Together.** Begin by singing all the verses of the Theme Song, "Life Is Good." Then review yesterday's discussion about greeting people.

Ask the children to open their books to pages 166 and 167 and review the story of Maria. Enjoy the illustrations with the children. Have them read the morning prayer on page 166 with you.

• Read page 168 with the children. After reading the first sentence, have the children complete the next four sentences that describe some things that we praise God for and that we ask God for. Elicit a response from each child to the first question. Have all the children draw a picture on page 168 of some way they will love and serve others. Let them share their drawings with the group.

Read about praying at night. Read page 169 and ask the children to name as many blessings of the day as they can recall. List these on a large sheet of posterboard on which you have printed the words *Thank You, God!* at the top. Talk with the children about the importance of ending each day in prayer. Explain that they can always talk to God in their own words telling God about everything that happened to them during the day. Have them read with you the prayer on page 169. Let them decorate it and challenge them to learn this prayer by heart.

◆ **Acting Justly.** Explain to the children that we owe God praise and thanksgiving for all the gifts of life we have received. Praise God each morning and thank God each night.

◆ **Praying Together.** Gather with the children in the prayer center. Prominently place the poster that lists their many blessings. Ask the children to close their eyes and listen very quietly as you slowly read the blessings listed on the poster. Pause after reading each blessing and invite the children to talk to God in their own hearts. Invite them to offer a quiet prayer of praise to God for each of the blessings. End by making the Sign of the Cross.

What is your favorite way to give praise to God?

How do you praise God during the week?

We praise God with all the gifts that God has given to us.

Day 4

◆ **Gathering Together.** Begin by singing all the verses of the Theme Song, "Life Is Good." Enjoy the gestures children can suggest. Have the children recall what they have learned about the wonderful gift of life. Tape a long roll of paper to the chalkboard. Invite the children to go through this chapter in their books, look at the pictures, and try to find words on each page that tell of the wonderful gifts God has given us.

List these gifts on the paper as the children name them. Be sure to include the most wonderful gift of all, that God made us to be like God. Comment on the beauty and variety of the animals God has made for our world. Have them notice the joyful expressions of the children in the pictures.

◆ **Sharing Together.** Have the children look back through this chapter again. This time ask them to note the title of each part. Have the children read these four titles together and encourage the children to remember them. Try to arouse great enthusiasm for this wonderful God who has been so good to us.

Ask the children to share with the group what their favorite lesson was during the past year. Give the children a chance to express at least one idea and ask them to tell why this was their favorite lesson. Share with the children what your own favorite story or lesson was and share why it was your favorite.

• Use page 171 to review and pull together the parts of this chapter.

• Tell the children that one of the ways we can thank God for life and for all the gifts we have received is by singing. Recall the melody they learned for the words "I am wonderfully made." Go over this song with them in preparation for their prayer service.

◆ **Acting Justly.** Tell the children how much you have enjoyed sharing your faith with them this year and share that you hope they will not forget God during the summertime. Encourage them to praise God at Sunday Mass, especially for all the blessings they have received during this past year. Remind them to ask God's blessing on their lives during the summer, especially during their morning and night prayers. Have the children name actions they will do to help others.

◆ **Praying Together.** Lead the children in the prayer celebration on page 170. Make this as joyful a celebration as possible. Follow the annotations.

You may wish to include the hymn "For the Beauty of the Earth" from the *Hymnal for Catholic Students,* #120.

Advent/Christmas

Journeying in Faith with Children

Aims

- To understand that Advent is a time for getting ready to celebrate Jesus' birth and life
- To remember and celebrate that Jesus is always with us.

New Words

Advent

Christmas

Emmanuel

Materials

- name cards: Advent, Christmas, Emmanuel
- red and green sheets of construction paper
- crayons, markers, and pencils
- various pictures
- envelopes

Gathering Together

◆ **Greet the children.** Greet each child warmly as he or she enters the room. You may wish to have a quiet recording of an Advent hymn playing in the background.

Sharing Together

◆ **Examine the picture.** Show the children a picture that portrays someone getting ready for an event. The event might be a birthday party, family meal, picnic, or a game. Talk with the children about what is happening in the picture, what event is being prepared for, and what they are doing to get ready.

◆ **Talk about Advent.** Show a name card with the word *Advent* printed in large letters. Have the children pronounce it after you. Ask if any of the children understand the meaning of the word. Then read the first two sentences on page 172 in their books. Ask the children the name of the day on which we celebrate Jesus' birthday. Show a name card for Christmas and point the date out on the calendar.

◆ **Remember Jesus' birth.** Show a picture of a family celebrating Christmas. Talk with the children about the picture and draw from them the real reason for our celebration of Christmas. Read the next paragraph on page 172. Show a name card with Emmanuel. Have the children repeat the name after you several times.

If you have a tape or recording of the traditional Advent song, "O Come, O Come, Emmanuel," this would be a good time to listen to it. Comment on what a beautiful word *Emmanuel* is because it tells us that God is right here with us in Jesus.

◆ **Make a poster.** Have a large poster prepared with a picture of Jesus in the center. Under the picture have the word *Emmanuel* traced out in large letters. Give each child an envelope with small pieces of different colored construction paper. Invite the children to fill in the word by pasting the pieces of construction paper inside the letters.

◆ **Learn about Advent.**   Read the rest of page 172 to the children. Ask them to follow along in the reading and listen for two things that we get ready during Advent. Then have them underline the last sentence on the page that tells what we remember during the time of Advent.

Acting Justly

◆ **Make a welcome card.**   Give each child a sheet of red or green construction paper and crayons. Ask each one to make a welcome card for Jesus that they can put by their Christmas tree or nativity scene at home. Suggest that they print the word *Welcome* on the inside of the card and color it. On the outside they can decorate the card with drawing and more coloring.

◆ **Pray together.**   Set the poster with the picture of Jesus and the decorated "Emmanuel" near the prayer table. Review the melody to the "Alleluia" learned during the year. Then conduct the prayer service on page 173.

Dear Catechist,

Faith is the word we use to describe our response to God's loving gift of self to us. Faith is what you as a catechist aim to strengthen and foster. As catechists, we provide opportunities for children to respond in faith. We cannot guarantee their response. As a free response faith cannot be demanded or programmed.

Faith is expressed in word and in deed. One way the church shows its faith is in service to others. Little children are not too young to be called to acts of justice. They need to be called to justice not only as individuals but as a community.

Children recognize ways in which others serve them. This recognition comes about through simple discussion and more fully through showing how others serve them. Through participation in audiovisual media, through creating their own visual expressions of love and service, through storytelling and role-playing, they can recognize service given and service being given.

As catechist, you can call children to service by creatively recognizing the many things that little children can do for others. Get-well cards, errands, and cleanup are only a few of the services these children can offer. Look around your neighborhood and parish to see what your children can do as a group. The important thing is that they recognize, as followers of Jesus, that they are called to be just and to serve others, especially those who are in need.

Sr. Anne Marie

EASTER

Journeying in Faith with Children

Aims

- To understand that each Sunday we celebrate the resurrection of Jesus
- To learn about Easter as a celebration of the resurrection of Jesus
- To learn about Easter as a time for baptisms

Materials

- Easter cards or pictures showing "new life"—eggs, chicks, birds, etc.
- Baptism photos

Gathering Together

◆ **Greet the children.** Show the children some Easter cards or pictures showing Easter eggs. Ask the children if they know why we receive eggs of many beautiful colors at Easter. Invite them to tell what happens when an egg is hatched. Show a picture of this, if possible. Explain that this is a reminder to us of the beginning of new life. On Easter we celebrate the beginning of new life in different ways.

Sharing Together

◆ **Learn about Jesus' resurrection** Explain that the egg is a reminder of Jesus' resurrection. After Jesus died on the cross for us, he came back to begin a new and wonderful life. We celebrate Jesus' resurrection every Sunday, but especially on Easter Sunday. Read to the children the first paragraph on page 174 of their books.

Continue the reading the next three paragraphs on page 174. Have the children sing an "Alleluia" that the parish uses at Mass or teach one with your own melody. Explain that this word is a special Easter word. Point out that Easter is one of the happiest times of the year for Jesus' followers because he rose from the dead on that day. Remember that Jesus promised that God will always be with us and will raise us someday to new life as well.

◆ **Show photographs of Baptism.** If you have a photo of someone in your family being baptized, share this with the children. If not, ask the children if they have ever seen a baptism. Have them tell you what they remember about it. Explain that Baptism makes us members of our community, the Church. Read the last two paragraphs on page 174.

◆ **Visit the baptismal font.** If it is possible, take the children to visit the baptismal font. Show them the basin that holds the water and explain something of the ritual of baptism. If you are unable to visit the font, show a picture of a child being baptized. Explain that each time a person is baptized they are already beginning a new life in Jesus. They share in the Easter life of Jesus.

Acting Justly

God will always be with us and will raise us someday to new life.

◆ **Renew baptismal vows.** Explain to the children that when they were baptized, their parents made promises to God for them. Your parents promised that you would always try to please God and not pay attention to anyone who would urge you to do wrong. Talk with the children about occasions when people have wanted them to do something bad. The children's parents promised that instead the children would do the right thing.

Recite a simple adaptation of the baptismal promises.

Catechist:	Do you promise to give up anything that is wrong?
Children:	Yes, we do.
Catechist:	Do you promise to try to keep away from anything that might make it easier for you to do something wrong?
Children:	Yes, we do.
Catechist:	Do you promise to always follow Jesus in your life, no matter how hard it might seem?
Children:	Yes, we do.

End by blessing each child with holy water.

Praying Together

◆ **Pray together.** Lead the children in the prayer celebration that appears on page 175.

LYRICS FOR *SONGS FOR LIVING WATERS 1*

MY NAME *by Stephen Chapin*

1. There's lots of kids, just like me and you,
   So how can we tell just who is who?
   We have our names for our whole life long
   To remind us of the family that we belong to.

Chorus:
   My name, everybody has one,
   My name, a first and a last one,
   My name, talking 'bout my name.
   My name, sounds so easy,
   Use my name, anytime you need me,
   Always the same, it's my name.
   I feel so proud, I shout it loud,
   It's my name.

2. We all belong to a family,
   The "Children of God," Christianity.
   We have our names for our whole life long
   To remind us of the family that we belong to.

Chorus

3. When we are young, we are all baptized
   With Christian names, named for Jesus Christ.
   We have our names for our whole life long
   To remind us of the family that we belong to.

Chorus

SPECIAL *by Stephen Chapin*

1. Every day I see other people who
   I can look up to, that's special.
   I have favorite girls, I have favorite boys,
   and my birthday toys they're special.

Chorus:
   If there's anyone you like seeing,
   If there's anyone you like being,
   If there's anyone in your mind
   Who's always kind to you,
   Then you know (clap, clap) what special people do.
   Special (clap, clap), so special (clap, clap),
   Like me (clap, clap), like you (clap, clap).
   Special (clap, clap), we're special (clap, clap),
   In all (clap, clap) we do (clap, clap, clap, clap).

2. Well, the Bible tells about Jesus Christ
   And the friends he had, that's special.
   He was always there when a friend would call,
   And he helped them all, that's special.

Chorus

3. Every Sunday is such a happy day
   When we sing and pray, that's special.
   When I go to church, where my family goes,
   In my Sunday clothes, that's special.

Chorus

HELPING HANDS *by Stephen Chapin*

Chorus:
   There's one, two, three, four, five
   Fingers on my left hand.
   There's one, two, three, four, five
   Fingers on my right hand.
   My ten fingers, so much fun,
   Can I make them work as one
   When it's time to do the best I can,
   When it's time to lend a helping hand.

1. Hands are for playing,
   Hands are for eating food with.
   Hands are for helping,
   Hands are for loving you with.
   Hands are for holding on
   Each time we might fall.
   Helping hands reaching out for us all.

Chorus

2. There was a man who lay
   On the roadside, bleeding.
   All of the people passed him
   And didn't see him.
   Then came a man who
   Lent a hand where he fell,
   And he helped him back home to get well.

Chorus

3. There was a man called
   Francis from Assisi.
   He was so rich his life
   Had become so easy.
   Then when a sick man
   Came and knocked at his door,
   Francis spent all his life with the poor.

Chorus

WE CAN HEAR *by Stephen Chapin*

1. There are sounds in the air,
   And we learn what they are.
   We can hear, we've got ears.
   There are words that we read;
   There are stories we learn.
   We can hear 'cause we've got ears.

Chorus:
   We can hear every bell when it's ringing.
   We can hear every song when we're singing,
   Singing low, singing high—high.
   We hear each other, sister and brother,
   We hear the world as it goes by.

2. Jesus says many things,
   And his words all are true.
   And we hear, we've got ears.
   He says, "Happy are those
   Who are working for peace,"
   And we hear 'cause we've got ears.

Chorus

3. Jesus says, "Love your God
   With your heart and your soul."
   And we hear, we've got ears.
   "And with all of your mind
   And your neighbor as well."
   And we hear 'cause we've got ears.

Chorus

OUR EYES *by Stephen Chapin*

Chorus:

> I look at you and you look at me.
> There is so much in the world
> We can see.
> We see the sun and the stars in the skies.
> We see the world that God made
> With our eyes.

1. Fish in the ocean,
   Birds in the trees,
   Flowers that bloom—
   God made all of these.
   Lakes full of water,
   Trees made of wood,
   See all these things,
   God is good.

Chorus

2. All that God's made,
   People are one.
   We are the best work
   That God has done.
   We know the right way;
   We care and give
   Love for the world where we live.

Chorus

3. Each Sunday morning
   When weekdays pass,
   We come together
   And go to Mass.
   People with people
   Come through the door,
   Helping the sick and the poor.

Chorus

LIFE IS GOOD *by Stephen Chapin*

Chorus:

    Life is good every day, every night, every way;
    We give thanks for the gifts we are given.
    Life is good every day, every night, every way;
    We give thanks for the world that we live in.

1. When we walk, that's living;
    When we're happy, living is such fun.
    When we talk, that's living;
    When we're happy, we tell everyone
    That life is fun.

Chorus

2. Breathe the air God gave us;
    When we're happy, living is such fun.
    Taste the food God gave us;
    When we're happy, we tell everyone
    That life is fun.

Chorus

3. Jesus says, "Be happy";
    When we're happy, living is such fun.
    We will all be happy;
    When we're happy, we tell everyone
    That life is fun.

Chorus

    (Repeat verse 1.)

Chorus

Refrains for Prayer Services

WE SING GOD'S PRAISES FOR - EV - ER.

JE - SUS YOU ARE THE SA - VIOUR. YOU ARE THE ONE SENT BY GOD.

I AM WON·DER·FUL·LY MADE. A - MEN A - MEN A - MEN.

IN THE NAME OF THE FA·THER, AND OF THE SON, AND OF THE HO·LY SPI·RIT A - MEN.